· CONCISE GUIDE TO ·

Colic in the Horse

Also by David W. Ramey, D.V.M.

Horsefeathers: Facts Versus Myths About Your Horse's Health

Concise Guide to Medications and Supplements for the Horse

Concise Guide to Tendon and Ligament Injuries in the Horse

Concise Guide to Navicular Syndrome in the Horse

· CONCISE GUIDE TO ·

Colic in the Horse

David W. Ramey, D.V.M.

Howell Book House
New York

Howell Book House
A Simon & Schuster Macmillan Company
1633 Broadway
New York, NY 10019

MACMILLAN is a registered trademark of Macmillan, Inc.

Library of Congress Cataloging-in-Publication Data

Ramey, David W.
        Concise guide to colic in the horse/David W. Ramey.
            p.   cm.
        Includes bibliographical references and index.
        ISBN 0-87605-911-6
        I. Colic in horses. I. Title.
SF959.C6R35   1996   96-11242
636.1'089755—dc20   CIP

Manufactured in the United States of America

10 9 8 7 6 5 4 3 2 1

CONTENTS

ACKNOWLEDGMENTS

It's sometimes difficult to communicate what you know to people. Medicine has its own language, which allows those who are educated in it to converse easily with one another. Any language, however, can become a barrier to adequate communication when both sides aren't equally well versed in it. The author of a book about horse medicine, for example, may understand what he is trying to say even if no one else does.

As in my first book, *Horsefeathers: Facts Versus Myths About Your Horse's Health*, the illustrations of Lynda Fenneman help make things clear. For their efforts in keeping things clear and understandable, three people and their helpful suggestions are readily and thankfully acknowledged. Patti Friedland is "beautiful and brilliant" as always. Sandra Sudduth found time to make helpful suggestions while keeping my veterinary practice running. Finally, to Beth, my wife, thanks for taking the time to read this book while still making time to do all the wonderful things you do to make my life great.

INTRODUCTION

Probably no condition of the horse is as feared by the horse owner as colic. Indeed, insurance companies report that colic (a condition generally thought of as some sort of abdominal disease) is one of the most frequently reported causes of death in the horse. Diseases of the horse's digestive system have been estimated to cause up to 50 percent of the medical problems of the horse! It is certainly understandable, then, why many owners seem preoccupied with the treatment and prevention of this condition.

Because colic is feared, many strategies have been devised to try to treat it and to avoid it. Some of the strategies have a sound medical foundation; others, unfortunately, would be more properly described as old wives' tales.

But what is colic? What causes it? Can it be prevented? What treatments are effective? What are the aftereffects? This book attempts to answer these and many other questions that owners have about colic. It should help the owner understand what is happening to the colicking horse and what to do about it. It should help the owner make an informed decision about and understand the treatment of his or her horse.

It will discuss some of the things (useful and otherwise) that are done in an effort to prevent colic.

Ideally, this guide will help allay some of the fears that horse owners have about this important condition. Believe it or not, colic is usually not that bad.

· CONCISE GUIDE TO ·

Colic in the Horse

CHAPTER I

Colic Defined

COLIC IS ONE OF THE OLDEST MEDICAL TERMS IN USE. The word comes from ancient Greece. Its classical Greek root refers specifically to the colon, the ending portion of the large intestine. In modern medical usage, *colic* is generally used as a generic term for pain that is thought to originate in the abdomen. In human medicine, the term is frequently used to describe nonspecific intestinal discomfort shown by infants.

In horse medicine, the word *colic* is used to mean the exact same thing as it does in people medicine. "Colic" pain as manifested by the horse can actually come from a variety of sources other than the intestines or the abdomen. Most commonly, though, when people refer to a colicking horse, they are thinking of a problem with the horse's intestines. They are also thinking of something bad for the horse.

Many conditions of the horse are associated with pain. The clinical appearance of these conditions can be confused with the pain that is caused by intestinal problems. So as to avoid confusion, in this book, when the word *colic* is used, it refers specifically to a condition of the horse's intestines. Other diseases that can be confused with primary intestinal problems will be identified as causing "colic-like pain." Many of these conditions are discussed in chapter five.

Colic is therefore not a specific term for a condition. It's much like the term *cancer*, which is used loosely to generalize a clinical condition rather than to detail specifically the condition itself. And as is the case with cancer, a diagnosis of colic can have many meanings. Cancer can be a diagnosis that refers to everything from a small, benign bump on your nose to a rapidly fatal disease process. Colic, too, can refer to everything from a condition that will pass in a few minutes to one that is ultimately fatal for the horse. *Without question, however, the vast majority of colics do not kill horses.*

True colics involving the intestines can be broadly divided into two groups: medical and surgical. A medical colic is one that will respond to treatment with medication and time (time is a very important part of the treatment of any disease). In this way, a medical colic is much like a stomachache in people. If, after a meal of rich food, your stomach is upset, you may find it helpful to lie down and take an antacid or something. Given a bit of time, digestion and medication, your discomfort will most likely pass. This sort of thing happens all the time to people; it happens all the time to horses, too.

Sometimes, however, colic discomfort can be a sign of a much more serious underlying condition. Using people as an example again, sometimes a sharp pain in the abdomen may indicate something bad, like appendicitis. Appendicitis is a very serious condition that most frequently requires surgical intervention. The fact is, if you need to get your appendix removed and it doesn't happen, you will die. Similarly, if a horse has a problem that requires surgical intervention and he doesn't get operated on, he will die.

This analogy can be pursued even further. Most people, if they get to the hospital in plenty of time and get their inflamed appendix removed, will recover without complications. But some unfortunate people will have complications, a few of which will even be fatal. Complications happen in medicine, sometimes even with the best of care.

Some horses that require surgery for their abdominal pain will not recover well from surgery, either. After all, surgery does present a risk to the horse. Anytime you take a risk (like crossing the street), you take a chance on not making it. Equine abdominal surgery is a very laborious, messy and involved process. But surgery is the only solution for some colic conditions of the horse if death is not an acceptable option, and many horses recover successfully from it.

Now that you understand what colic is, the next step to understanding it is to "look inside" the normal horse to see from where colic problems may arise.

CHAPTER 2

The Abdomen of the Normal Horse

THE HORSE'S ABDOMEN IS A BIG CAVITY THAT, IN REALity, has only a very few things inside it. The abdomen is bordered on the front by the diaphragm, the big muscle that pumps the lungs. On all other sides, the abdomen is defined by the various muscles of the ribs and abdomen. The largest structures within the abdominal cavity are the liver, urinary bladder, spleen, large and small intestines, stomach, pancreas and, in the female, the reproductive organs. (The kidneys are actually just above the abdominal cavity, and horses don't have a gall bladder.) The typical signs of colic can be associated with many different diseases. For example, any of the various abdominal organs can be associated with clinical signs of colic (although the pancreas is almost never reported as having problems in the horse). In general usage, however, when people think of a colic, they are usually referring to a condition of the horse's intestines.

Structures such as the liver, kidneys, reproductive organs, bladder, pancreas and spleen occupy relatively fixed positions in the horse. The rest of the abdomen is filled with structures that can shift position and move around, primarily the intestinal tract and its mesentery (see figures 1 and 2). (The mesentery supports the intestines, and through it run various blood vessels and lymph nodes.) In fact, it is the mobility of the intestines that often gets them into trouble—sort of like young boys with cars. Finally, the abdominal cavity is lined by the peritoneum, a strong colorless membrane.

THE ABDOMINAL CAVITY

This section on the anatomy of the abdominal cavity is not intended to be comprehensive. Instead, it is only meant to give you an idea of where the largest and most important structures in the abdomen are. Much more detail about the anatomy of the horse's abdomen can be found in texts on equine anatomy. The interested reader is encouraged to consult them for additional facts.

The Liver

The liver sits in the very front of the horse's abdomen, just behind the muscular diaphragm. A very large organ, the liver takes up the whole front part of the horse's abdominal cavity.

The liver has many important roles in the horse's body, including the filtration of the blood, the secretion of bile (important for normal diges-tion) and the excretion of bilirubin (a by-product of the breakdown of old blood cells that are removed from circulation) and other substances formed at other sites in the body. The liver also has numerous metabolic functions. Normal functioning of the liver is essential to life.

· Figure I ·

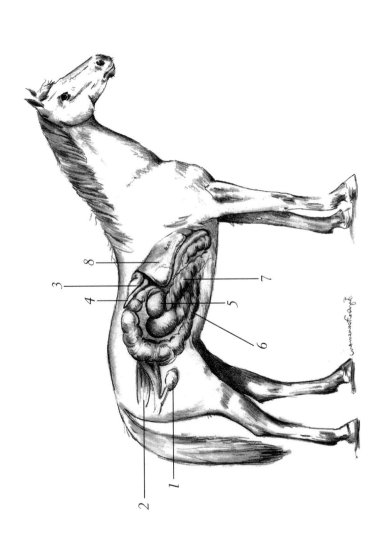

From the horse's right side, structures that can be identified are these: (1) urinary bladder; (2) rectum; (3) right kidney; (4) duodenum; (5) base of cecum; (6) apex of cecum; (7) large colon and (8) liver.

The Kidneys

There are two kidneys in the horse. They lie in the lumbar region of the back (toward the back of the horse, underneath where the back of a saddle sits), below the back muscles and on either side of the spine. The left kidney is a bit farther back towards the tail than is the right kidney. (This allows for part of the left kidney to be examined during a routine rectal examination.) Both kidneys lie just outside the abdominal cavity itself (above and outside of the peritoneum).

The kidneys filter the blood and excrete the end products of the body's metabolism in the form of urine. They also regulate the concentrations of the various salts in the body fluids of the horse.

The Pancreas

The pancreas is an elongated gland that runs alongside the first segment of the horse's small intestines (the duodenum). It lies in the front part of the horse's abdomen, on the right side.

The pancreas secretes enzymes into the intestines which are very important for normal digestive function. In addition, the pancreas controls the secretion of insulin, a hormone that is critical to the regulation of blood sugars.

The Bladder, Ureters and Urethra

The bladder is a membranous sac in the back part of the horse's abdomen that serves as a collecting vessel for the urine that is produced by the horse's kidneys. It is connected to each kidney by a ureter, a thin, membranous tube (though extremely rare, problems with the ureters have also been reported as a cause of colic-like pain in the horse). The bladder narrows into the urethra. The urethra connects the bladder to the outside so that the urine formed by the kidneys can be eliminated.

· Figure 2 ·

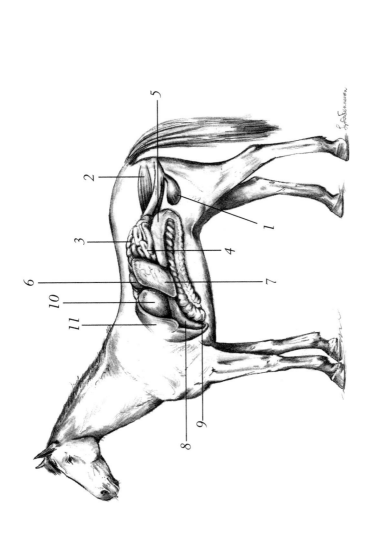

From the horse's left side, structures that can be identified are these: (1) urinary bladder; (2) rectum; (3) small colon; (4) jejunum; (5) pelvic flexure of the left colon; (6) left kidney; (7) spleen; (8) diaphragmatic flexure of the large colon; (9) sternal flexure of the large colon; (10) stomach and (11) liver.

The Reproductive Tract (Mare)

The internal reproductive tract of the mare consists of the ovaries, the uterus, the cervix and the vagina. The cervix and the vagina, however, do not lie within the abdomen itself. The reproductive structures are in the back of the abdomen and lie above the urinary bladder. Imagine that you are standing behind the mare: The reproductive tract is laid out like the letter *T*, with the vertical line of the T being the cervix, vagina and the body of the uterus. The horizontal line of the T is the "horns" of the uterus. One of the two ovaries lies at each end of the horizontal line of the T.

The Reproductive Tract (Stallion)

The primary reproductive organs of the male horse, the testicles, lie outside of the abdominal cavity, in a sack called the scrotum. They didn't start out there, though.

In the fetal horse, the reproductive structures all start out in the same place, up under the spine of the fetus, near the kidneys. In the female horse, the structures stay put. In the male horse, however, the testicles must descend through a slit on either side of the abdomen before finally coming to rest in the scrotum.

The slit in the abdomen through which the testicles, their blood vessels and muscles pass is known as the inguinal ring. In stallions, the inguinal ring is a very important structure. Loops of intestines can occasionally pass through the inguinal ring and get caught in the scrotum (this is called an inguinal hernia).

The Spleen

The spleen normally lies on the left side of the horse's abdomen, against the body wall. It's a very large organ and the back edge of the spleen can be felt during a rectal examination. The spleen is somewhat mobile and is not firmly attached in its place in the abdomen. Therefore, it can become involved in certain colic conditions.

The spleen has vital functions in red blood cell metabolism. It also serves as an important storage reservoir for red blood cells in the horse. Horses can literally double the number of red blood cells in their circulation due to contraction of the spleen.

THE INTESTINAL TRACT

The intestinal tract is a long tube that, if you think about it, is really isolated from the rest of the horse's body. That is, there is an opening at the mouth and another opening at the rear end of the horse, but the contents of the tube are never in contact with any of the other internal structures of the horse. Thus, things taken in by the horse have to be processed by the intestines before they can be used by the horse's body.

The intestinal tract of the horse is more than 100 feet long. (See figure 3.) Who knows, perhaps that's one reason why it's prone to so many problems! Although the intestinal tract is a continuous tube, it actually consists of a number of continuous segments.

The Stomach

The stomach of the horse is shaped somewhat like the letter *J*. It lies in the upper front part of the abdomen and cannot be felt by rectal palpation.

Unlike most mammals, horses are unable to regurgitate feed or liquid from their stomachs. The main reason for this is thought to be, at least partially, the shape of the stomach. When the stomach fills, it sort of closes off the opening to the top. Material cannot go back up towards the mouth.

· FIGURE 3 ·

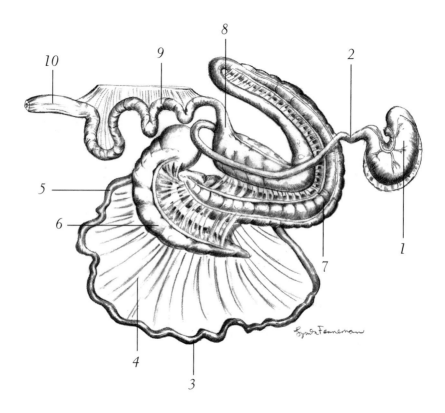

Laid out from end to end, the horse's intestinal tract consists of (1) the stomach; (2) the duodenum; (3) the jejunum; (4) the supporting mesentery; (5) the ileum; (6) the cecum; (7) the segments of the large colon; (8) the transverse colon; (9) the small colon and (10) the rectum.

This has very important implications in colic. If the horse's stomach gets too full, from impactions of feed or from fluid buildup in the small intestine that lies beyond, the stomach can rupture from the pressure. If the stomach does tear, fluid may then be regurgitated through the mouth or nose. Unfortunately, stomach rupture is a fatal condition in horses.

The stomach secretes acid and enzymes (gastric juices) that are important in the first stages of digestion. The stomach leads into the small intestine.

The Small Intestine

The small intestine takes up a lot of room in the horse's abdomen and there's a lot of small intestine in the horse. The small intestine makes up approximately 75 percent of the total length of the intestinal tract.

The small intestine, which can be as long as 75 feet, has many important digestive functions. The digestive processes of the small intestine occur because of enzymes that are secreted by the lining of the intestine. Normal digestion also depends on other secretions, which are deposited in the intestines from the liver and the pancreas. Fats, sugars and proteins (which are all components of the feed that horses eat) are broken down and absorbed in the small intestine.

The small intestine of the horse is divided into three segments. In order of appearance, they are the following:

The Duodenum   The front segment of the small intestine, 3 to 5 feet in length. This part of the small intestine is relatively fixed in position in the upper front part of the abdomen.

The Jejunum   The middle segment of the small intestine, comprising 50 to 70 feet of its total 75-foot length. Most of the jejunum lies in the upper part of the left half of the horse's abdomen, where it is mixed up with coils of the small colon.

The jejunum is suspended in the abdomen by the mesentery, a filmy tissue that originates under the spine. Through the mesentery run all the blood vessels of the intestine. The position of the jejunum is not at all fixed in the abdomen. The normal muscular activity of this highly mobile part of the small intestine gets it into all sorts of trouble. Because it is so long and can move around, the jejunum is susceptible to twisting, to getting trapped in small spaces and to telescoping on itself (this is called intussusception).

The Ileum   The end segment of the small intestine, the ileum is only 2 to 3 feet in length. The ileum is more muscular than other parts of the small intestine. Its position is relatively fixed in the abdomen. The ileum joins into the first part of the large intestine, the cecum, in the right side of the horse's abdomen.

The Large Intestine

The large intestine is so named because—you guessed it—it is so much larger in diameter than the small intestine. The various parts of the large intestine comprise about 25 percent of the total length of the intestinal tract.

The large intestine also has important digestive functions. It works quite differently from the small intestine. The large intestine does not have enzymes produced by the lining of the bowel to aid in digestion. Rather, the large intestine has an active and flourishing population of bacteria and other microorganisms. These microbes break down feedstuffs primarily by a well-known process called fermentation (the same process used to make beer and other alcoholic beverages).

Enzyme activity by the bacteria in the large intestine causes fermentation of the horse's feed, especially the carbohydrate portions of the feed. Enzyme activity helps break down feed into simple sugars, which are then absorbed by the intestine to provide energy for the horse's body. Bacterial enzyme activity allows the horse to digest and use feeds that are impossible for simple-stomached mammals (like people) to process, such as hay.

Fermentation produces, as a by-product of the process, large amounts of gas. The gas must be removed by normal movement of the intestines. Since the fermentation activity occurs near the end of the intestinal tract, horses are normally quite flatulent. (Cows, which ferment in the front part of their intestinal tract, burp a lot.)

If the normal movement of the large intestine is disrupted, it can cause the bowel to fill up with gas. Also, when the large bowel is twisted or obstructed, as fermentation proceeds, gas can build up behind the problem. Gas accumulation can cause a great deal of pain for the horse because it stretches the bowel. "Rich" feeds, such as grains or very green hay, which are high in carbohydrates, can also cause excessive production of gas due to bacterial fermentation.

The Cecum   The cecum is the initial part of the large intestine in the horse. It is approximately 3 feet long and shaped like a comma. The cecum is blind-ended, that is, it sits out like a thumb off the intestinal tract. The cecum is very much like the human appendix. It's a cul-de-sac off of the main street that is the intestinal tract. The cecum occupies primarily the right side of the horse's abdomen.

The Large Colon   The large colon of the horse is a huge structure that makes up about 10 feet of the total 25-foot length of the large intestine. It begins on the right side of the abdomen, at the base of the cecum, and occupies the floor of the abdomen. The large colon is laid into the abdomen in large loops, which lay on top of each other like two horseshoes.

The large colon is divided into four segments. The names of the segments describe the position of the various portions. The first segment of the large colon is the right ventral, which travels forward towards the horse's head (in the horse, ventral means toward the ground). It then loops back at the diaphragm (the curve of the horseshoe) into the left ventral colon. The loop at this level is called the sternal flexure, since it's up by the horse's sternum. The left ventral colon travels back towards the horse's tail, where it then loops back up on top of itself, forming the left dorsal colon (in the horse's abdomen, dorsal means up towards the back). The upward loop of the colon in this area is called the pelvic flexure. (The pelvic flexure can usually be felt during rectal examination, and it is a common area where feed or other material can become impacted.) The left dorsal colon then travels forward again, making another horseshoe-shaped curve at the diaphragm; this curve is called the diaphragmatic flexure. After the right turn at the diaphragm, the large colon then is called the right dorsal colon.

The positions of segments of the large colon in the abdomen are very important. Unfortunately for the horse, however, these segments are not fixed into position. Just like the jejunum of the small intestine, these segments can move around in the abdomen. Changes in position of the various segments of the large intestine are associated with all sorts of colic problems. If the segments get out of position, somebody has to go in and put them back.

The Transverse Colon The right dorsal colon terminates in a small, short, constricted portion of the large colon called the transverse colon. This part of the large intestine is so named because it runs from the right to the left side of the horse's abdomen, transversely across the abdomen. The transverse colon is in the front portion of the abdomen, roughly at the level of the 17th or 18th rib, and it is closely associated with the pancreas. The transverse colon is firmly fixed in position. It cannot be felt during a rectal examination.

The transverse colon is another site where impactions of feed or enteroliths (stones) commonly occur. This is thought to be because the transverse colon is much narrower than the right dorsal colon that feeds into it. It's an obvious place for things to get stuck in the intestinal tract, as the diameter of the bowel goes from large to small.

The Small Colon   The small colon is so called because of its small diameter relative to the rest of the large intestine. It's a fairly long segment of large intestine, up to 13 feet in length. The small colon leaves the transverse colon and winds its way to the back of the horse through the upper left part of the abdomen. There, it gets mixed in with coils of the jejunem of the small intestine.

Although the small colon is somewhat mobile, it rarely has problems with twists. The most commonly seen problems of the small colon are impactions of material or obstruction by enteroliths (stones).

The Rectum   The rectum is the short terminal part of the large intestine, only 2 to 3 feet in length. The rectum is rarely involved in colic problems unless it becomes torn. Rectal tears occur usually as a result of rectal examination, but they can also occur with no obvious or apparent cause.

CHAPTER 3

The Signs of Colic

OBVIOUSLY, THE MOST EASILY RECOGNIZED SIGN OF COLIC in the horse is pain. Most people can immediately recognize that a horse is feeling pain. They know that something is wrong with the horse.

The horse demonstrates colic pain in a number of ways, many of which are quite dramatic. Most obviously, colicking horses look like they are uncomfortable. Most horses are not stoic about pain and will usually let you know that they hurt. (See figure 4.)

Horses react to pain by pawing the ground or looking back at their abdomen, as if they are trying to point out to you where the pain is coming from. They may curl their upper lip. They may get up and down frequently, as if trying to find a position that is comfortable for them (sort of like when you curl up on the couch). It is also not at all uncommon for a horse with colic pain to begin to sweat. When the pain is more severe, horses may roll around or thrash on the ground, as if they are trying desperately to get away from the pain. (When a horse rolls around on the ground, the rolling does not threaten to "twist" the intestines, by the way; more on this in chapter 6.)

· FIGURE 4 ·

Signs associated with colic.

buckling or getting up and down

stretching

rolling and thrashing

pawing

kicking or biting at the sides

curling the upper lip

Other horses may appear to be paralyzed by their pain. These horses will stand and tremble, almost as if they are gritting their teeth through the ache in their abdomen. In the author's experience, many of the horses that demonstrate this type of pain have serious conditions that require surgical correction.

Male horses with colic will occasionally stretch out and even lower their penises. Some people mistakenly interpret this sign of pain as an inability to urinate.

Colicking horses will generally refuse to eat, although horses with mild or intermittent pain may eat halfheartedly or intermittently. If a horse colics and still wants to eat, more often than not it is a good sign, in the author's experience.

Most importantly, even if you do not immediately recognize that your horse has a colic, you will know that something is wrong with him or her. Many owners underestimate their ability to recognize that something is wrong with their horse. You know your horse better than anyone. If you think something is wrong with your horse, there most likely is. If your horse starts to "act funny" or doesn't want to eat, watch him carefully to make sure that he doesn't start to show some of the more obvious signs of colic.

Many other medical conditions can be confused with acute colic referable to intestinal problems in the horse. A number of diseases can be associated with vague or mild signs of colic-like pain. For example, pleuritis or pleuropneumonia, an infection of the horse's thoracic cavity ("shipping fever"), can cause a horse to be generally uncomfortable and not eat. Laminitis, an inflammatory condition of the feet, can make a horse reluctant to stand or move. Disease of the liver or kidneys can make a horse lose its appetite or show mild signs of discomfort. Peritonitis, an infection of the abdominal cavity, can also produce signs of mild pain that mimic those associated with intestinal colic. These and many other examples are listed in the following chapters.

Because colic is not a specific condition and many other maladies have clinical signs that can be mistaken for signs of acute intestinal colic, it is important that a horse with clinical signs of colic be evaluated by your veterinarian. He or she will then undertake one of a number of diagnostic steps in an effort to determine exactly what is wrong with your horse.

CHAPTER 4

The Diagnosis of Colic

ALTHOUGH THE VAST MAJORITY OF COLICS IN THE HORSE are not life-threatening, you should pay attention to them. Once you (or your neighbor) have recognized that your horse has a colic, you should call your veterinarian. Your veterinarian will come to gather a bunch of clinical data to help him or her evaluate how severe the colic is. Your veterinarian will then prescribe some sort of treatment.

In reality, there is ultimately only one important decision that needs to be made about the horse with colic. It must be decided as quickly as possible whether the colicking horse has a condition that requires medical or surgical treatment. If a horse has a "medical" colic, he will most likely respond to treatment at the farm or stable where he is located. The response to treatment may not necessarily be quick. Your horse may require several visits by the veterinarian or even hospitalization in severe cases.

If, however, the horse has a condition that requires surgical correction, this needs to be recognized as quickly as possible. If the horse is a candidate for surgery, he should be as healthy as possible. A horse that is in shock and has dead or dying tissue inside its abdomen is much less likely to have a successful recovery from colic surgery than a horse that gets to surgery before serious complicating factors begin. If your horse needs it, the most important way to help ensure the best recovery *from* surgery is to get him *into* surgery as quickly as you can.

The rapid and accurate diagnosis of colic is part art, part science and part experience. Your veterinarian will assess many variables in the diagnosis of your horse's colic. Each bit of information will give him or her some idea of how serious the problem really is.

CLINICAL HISTORY

The clinical history of the horse with colic can be very helpful in giving hints as to what the cause of his condition might be. Feeding and housing conditions may help point to the underlying cause of the horse's colic pain. For example, a horse that is kept in an environment where exposure to sand is possible would be suspect for a colic induced by sand in the intestines. Similarly, poor quality or extremely rich feed in the horse's feeder may suggest a reason for an indivdual horse's colic.

The horse's previous medical history should also be considered. A horse with a history of a previous abdominal surgery might eventually have additional problems related to his surgery. A horse with a poor history of control of internal parasites might possibly have colic problems related to them. Similarly, the medical history of other horses in the barn may be important; abdominal pain in one horse may be associated with episodes of illness in other horses. For example, horses with conditions such as streptococcus infections (strangles) may develop abscesses inside their abdomen, with resulting pain and colic-like signs. Other infectious diseases such as ehrlichiosis (Potomac horse fever) or infectious diarrheas caused by the *Salmonella* bacteria can also cause colic-like pain.

The sex and breeding history of the horse must also be noted. The uterus of a pregnant mare can twist late in pregnancy and cause severe colic-like pain. In stallions, intestines may become entrapped in the scrotal or inguinal areas and cause severe colics.

Curiously, the weather is often implicated as a cause of colic. Many people believe that any change in the weather is accompanied by an increased incidence of colic. Several studies have been performed to see whether there is any association between changes in the weather and episodes of colic. So far, no such relationship has been found. People always talk about it, though.

PAIN

Pain itself can be useful in determining the severity of the horse's colic. As a general rule, the more severe the pain, the more potentially serious the colic. Horses that have mild or occasional pain accompanied by few physiological changes are much less likely to have a serious problem than horses with severe, uncontrollable pain whose condition is deteriorating.

However, there are certainly dramatic exceptions to this rule. Some horses (like some people) don't seem to tolerate pain well at all. Others show only mild discomfort even when suffering from the most severe problems. Horses with serious problems that require surgery are frequently in great pain, but they may only stand stiffly, as if paralyzed by the ache in their abdomen.

If colic pain is difficult to control or does not go away after one or more treatments, this may be an indication that the colic is serious. The two most potent pain-relieving agents for colic—xylazine and detomodine—normally control pain for approximately twenty and sixty minutes, respectively. The failure of either of these agents to control the pain of a colic for more than a few minutes is generally a sign that the problem is of a more severe type. *Unrelenting and uncontrollable pain in a colicking horse is usually an indication that a horse's colic problem is surgical.*

Certain physiological stimuli are associated with the production of abdominal pain in the horse. Chief among them is the stretching of the intestines.

When the intestines are enlarged beyond their normal diameter, the horse reacts with a painful response. In experiments, colics can be caused by putting a balloon in the horse's intestines and inflating it. Methane gas, which is produced by the normal bacterial action in the large intestines as a by-product of fermentation, acts just like a balloon in producing colic pain. Gas buildup can occur as a result of too much fermenting activity (from very rich or green hay, for example). Gas accumulation is also caused by blockage in or around the intestines, which allows gas to build up behind the obstructed area. Obstructions of the intestines by feed or other material can also cause distension of the bowel. Pain is the end result.

Impairment of the circulation to the intestines is also painful to the horse. When the intestines are twisted, entrapped or strangulated, blood continues to pump into the intestines, but it cannot flow out. Blood flows into the intestines via arteries, which have a significant amount of pressure in them. The pressure can force blood into the compromised or twisted area of intestines. Veins, on the other hand, which take the blood out of an area, have very little pressure in them. Their flow is easily obstructed. Thus, blood can actually build up and stagnate in the wall of the affected area of intestines, causing swelling and death of the intestines along with the clinical signs of pain.

While pain is certainly the most common indicator of colic in the horse, not all horses that demonstrate signs of pain have an intestinal problem. For example, inflammation or infections in the abdomen (peritonitis) can cause colic pain. (Fortunately, abdominal infection and inflammation is a relatively uncommon occurrence in the horse.) Nor do all horses with colic-like pain necessarily even have an abdominal problem. Other painful conditions such as pleuritis, laminitis, lymphosarcoma (a type of cancer) and myositis (tying-up or exertional rhabdomyolysis) have been mistaken for intestinal colic in the horse.

Fever

Fever, an elevation in the horse's normal body temperature, is not usually associated with colic or abdominal pain. Fever is most commonly associated with infection of one thing or another. Most painful conditions of the abdomen of the horse are not caused by infections and hence are not usually accompanied by fevers. The horse's normal temperature is between 99.5 and 101 degrees Farenheit.

If fever is seen in association with colic or colic-like pain, however, it always indicates that aggressive diagnostic action should be taken to determine the source of the fever. Fever in a horse that shows signs of colic can be associated with many serious infectious conditions, such as peritonitis, abdominal abscess, rupture of the intestines or pleuropneumonia. These are conditions that must be treated very aggressively. Unfortunately, these diseases often have fatal consequences.

Heart Rate and Pulse

The resting pulse of the normal horse is usually between 32 and 44 beats per minute. The rate is higher in ponies and foals; it can be a little lower in very athletic horses. The pulse can be taken at one of a variety of locations on the horse's face or legs; your veterinarian can show you where to find it most easily. It's also easy to pick up the horse's heart rate by listening to the heart with a stethoscope.

Pain causes the heart rate to elevate. It usually elevates in proportion to the amount of pain. Thus, the most painful and serious colics are typically associated with a greatly increased pulse rate, often to more than 60 beats a minute or more. The pulse rate will also elevate when the horse goes into the early stages of shock. Shock is a complex metabolic condition that results from the body's attempt to maintain circulation to the most vital areas of the body, such as the brain and heart.

Colicking horses with pulse rates that stay around normal usually do not require surgery. Pulse rates of more than 60 beats per minute, particularly if they cannot be controlled by pain-relieving medication, are frequently a sign that aggressive intervention, either medically, surgically or both, may be required.

RESPIRATION RATE

The respiration rate may also increase when the horse is experiencing colic pain. Rapid or shallow respirations are commonly seen in all mammals in response to painful stimuli. The normal horse breathes from ten to twenty times per minute.

Rapid, shallow respirations in a horse that demonstrates mild signs of colic should not necessarily be taken as a sign of abdominal pain, however. Some horses with infectious conditions of the chest or lungs can demonstrate colic-like pain that is almost indistinguishable from pain originating from the intestines. Horses with pleuropneumonia (shipping fever), seen most commonly after a horse is transported, occasionally have signs that mimic colic. Importantly, these horses frequently have fevers, as well. Similar signs of vague pain have also been demonstrated by horses with tumors of the chest cavity; many times these horses will have increased respiration, too (these conditions are really rare).

MUCOUS MEMBRANES (GUMS)

The horse's gums reflect his circulatory status. The smallest blood vessels, the capillaries, are very close to the surface in the horse's mouth. Thus, the gums have a pink hue because of the red blood that runs through them. The health of the horse's circulation, as reflected in the gums, can be a good indicator of the horse's overall metabolic state.

Commonly, when the colicking horse is examined, the capillary refill time is checked. If thumb pressure is put on the gums and then removed, a white thumbprint can be briefly seen. This is because blood has been pushed out of the underlying capillaries (small blood vessels). This thumbprint should disappear in less than two seconds (this is called a capillary refill test).

Be precise if you're doing a capillary refill test on your colicking horse. In the author's experience, people have a tendency to forget how long two seconds really is. In their excitement and concern for their sick horse, many people count quickly "one-two" and think that their horse's refill time is increased. if you make sure you do the test properly, you'll save yourself a lot of anxiety.

Changes in the normal appearance of the gums are associated with shock and dehydration. These are serious complications in the colicking horse. When the horse begins to go into shock or is significantly dehydrated, the circulation is diverted away from less critical areas of the body, such as the gums and the legs, in favor of more critical areas such as the heart and brain. This change in circulatory priorities is reflected in the gums. As fluid is diverted to more critical areas in shock and dehydration, the gums also begin to dry out. If changes in the gums are noted, large amounts of intravenous fluids may be required to help the horse maintain his circulation.

In the inital stages of shock, the capillary refill time may actually be shortened. This is because early in shock, the heart begins to pump faster in an effort to keep up the delivery of blood. As shock progresses, the refill time becomes prolonged. This indicates that the system is beginning to fail to deliver blood to the less critical areas of the horse's body.

The gums also change color as shock progresses. Normally, the gums are a light salmon pink in color. The color of the gums change from pink, to red, to pale, to blue, to purple with the progression of shock. This is because as the circulation slows, all the oxygen gets sucked out of the normally red blood cells. Blood that has lots of oxygen in it is red; blood that has had the oxygen removed is very dark. Dry or sticky, blue or purple gums with prolonged capillary refill time indicate circulatory collapse. Gums like this mean that the horse's body is unable to maintain itself. Such signs are associated with a grave prognosis.

SKIN PINCH TEST

The pinch test is a commonly used test to assess dehydration in the horse. It's used a lot because it's really easy to do. In the skin pinch test, a "pinch" of skin is lifted from the neck of the horse. If the skin quickly returns to its normal shape after it is pinched, this is interpreted as a good sign. Conversely, if the skin remains in its pinched position, this is commonly thought to be a sign that the horse is dehydrated. (Dehydration occurs in the colicking horse as he goes into shock. Horses that colic also usually refuse to drink, which adds to the problem.)

Unfortunately, this test is not nearly as useful as people think. Many normal horses will have skin that does not return quickly to its normal shape. Conversely, in horses that really are dehydrated, the skin pinch test is not a very sensitive indicator of dehydration. Evaluation of the gums is a bit better indicator of dehydration than the skin pinch test. Although just about everyone can figure out how to do it, the skin pinch test has little true diagnostic value in evaluating the colicking horse.

ABDOMINAL SOUNDS

The normal horse's abdomen makes a lot of noise. Sometimes the sounds are so loud that they can be heard from across the stall! These sounds are associated with the normal propulsive movement of the intestines from the mouth to the rear.

When performing colic examinations, veterinarians listen to both sides of the horse's abdomen. The mere presence of abdominal sounds does not mean that the intestines are moving normally, however. Furthermore, sounds from one side or another do not give an indication as to what part of the intestines is involved in the colic problem. In the horse with intestinal colic problems, the groans and growls that indicate progressive abdominal movement are frequently depressed or nonexistent. This only reflects the fact that the intestines are not moving normally.

The lack of sounds from the abdomen does not necessarily mean that things are really serious for the colicking horse. Horse owners get scared to death that because the intestinal sounds aren't normal, the horse is going to die. In fact, a variety of stimuli can cause the horse's intestines to make fewer sounds, including exercise, excitement, infection and inflammation.

If normal abdominal sounds are present in a horse that shows signs of colic, it is generally a good sign, even though it does not mean that the horse is safe from serious trouble. Certainly, in a colicking horse in which no normal sounds were present when the horse first became sick, the return of normal sounds can generally be interpreted as a positive sign of recovery.

Some sounds coming from the abdomen are even associated with specific colic conditions. For example, gas in the intestines has its own characteristic sound. Gas gives a hollow or ringing sound to the intestines that is quite unforgettable once it has been heard for the first time. Additionally, areas of gas-distended bowel can resound with a "ping" when the overlying skin is thumped with the fingers. (This is due to the echo of the thump across the stretched-out walls of the gut.) Also, on occasion, the sound of sand in the intestine has been described as that of sand being poured.

RECTAL EXAMINATION

A thorough rectal examination is essential for the adequate evaluation of the horse with colic. In some cases, a specific diagnosis of the cause of the horse's colic can be made by rectal examination. In most cases, however, rectal exam findings must be combined with the other bits of information that are gathered during the physical examination to help make a diagnosis.

The back part of the horse's abdomen is all that can be examined during a rectal examination. It should be remembered that only about 40 percent of the abdomen can be examined in a rectal exam; structures such as the stomach, liver and the right kidney are out of reach of even the longest arms. On the horse's left side, the examiner usually can feel the various structures of the large and small colon, the back edge of the spleen and the back of the left kidney. On the right side, the examiner most often feels the cecum, (the large blind sac that is similar to but much larger than the human appendix). The bladder can also be felt in the posterior abdomen. In the female, the reproductive structures are easily felt; in the male it is possible to palpate the inguinal rings.

Many horses are surprisingly tolerant of rectal examinations. However, if a horse resists a rectal exam, he must be adequately restrained or sedated. This is both to protect the examiner from getting kicked and to help reduce the risk of tearing or damaging the horse's rectum during the examination.

Defecation and Fecal Examination

The feces should also be examined during a rectal exam. Ideally, fecal material should be present in the rectum and be of normal consistency and odor. The presence of dark blood in the manure suggests bleeding somewhere in the intestines; the presence of fresh, red blood suggests that the rectum has been torn or damaged during the exam. If a horse is heavily parasitized, sometimes, to the dismay of the examiner, parasites will be seen on the rectal exam glove when it is withdrawn. Mucus on the feces is often seen when the fecal material is passing through the intestines more slowly than normal. Mucus in feces sort of makes the feces look like it has been mixed with large noodles.

In areas where it is likely to occur, the feces should also be examined for the presence of sand. Sand is a common cause of impaction of the intestines in horses that live in a sandy environment. Feces removed from the rectum can be mixed with water to make a slurry; the heavy sand will settle to the bottom of a bucket or rectal examination sleeve. If sand is observed in the manure, treatment for sand accumulation is warranted. (You can check your horse's manure for the presence of sand yourself by taking feces from a fresh pile of feces and mixing it with water in a bucket. Make sure that you don't scoop up sand from the ground when you do this test, however, or else your test results will not be accurate.)

Diarrhea can also be associated with signs of colic. Sand in the intestines can cause diarrhea as well as impaction. Sand irritates the intestines, and they respond by secreting water. Too much water in the intestines causes diarrhea.

Infectious diarrheas, those that are normally caused by bacteria in the horse, are also associated with signs of colic-like pain. Colic signs in horses with diarrhea are due to the inflammation in the intestines and the excessive production of gas by the infecting bacteria. Some horses with infectious diarrheas can get very sick. They can require aggressive medical therapy with intravenous fluids and antibiotics in an effort to return them to good health.

If no feces are present in the rectum during a rectal exam, it suggests that things aren't moving very well in the abdomen. Many colic conditions can cause a lack of feces in the rectum. If fecal material continues to be absent in the rectum on follow-up examinations of the colicking horse, it may be one indication that surgical intervention is required. Conversely, if progressive movement of manure is seen in colicking horses during subsequent examinations, it is usually a very good sign.

Defecation is commonly seen in horses with colic, especially early in the condition. Horses with colic frequently strain and evacuate any fecal matter that is present in the rectum. This type of defecation early in colic does not necessarily reflect normal intestinal movement. In fact, it only indicates that there was manure in the last three feet of the intestines at the time the colic started. However, defecation and a reduction in pain as a colic episode subsides are always good signs.

NASOGASTRIC TUBE (STOMACH TUBE)

Passing a flexible tube through the nasal passages of the horse and down into the stomach is useful for both the diagnosis and treatment of colic. Passing a tube into the stomach can also relieve gas and fluid accumulation and the resulting discomfort that they cause.

Why pass the tube through the horse's nostril instead of its mouth? Well, the main reason is that a tube can't be passed through the horse's mouth if the horse is awake. The anatomy of the horse's mouth and the muscles of the tongue make it difficult for a tube to go through the mouth and down the esophagus (see figure 5). In addition, the horse's temperament makes it impossible to shove a tube down its mouth. The nostril is used because it is a convenient and relatively easy route through which to pass the tube.

The use of a nasogastric tube as a diagnostic tool is indicated in almost all cases of colic. It is especially important if the colic appears to be severe or to require surgery. Significant amounts of fluid or gas can accumulate in the stomach of a colicking horse. This most commonly happens when the small intestine is obstructed. If fluid can't pass through the small intestine, it backs up behind the obstruction, causing pain (from stretching of the bowel) and threatening rupture of the stomach.

Passing a tube into the stomach can help to relieve gas and fluid accumulation. This helps make the horse feel better. Even more importantly, a nasogastric tube in the stomach can help prevent stomach rupture. Stomach rupture is a fatal condition for the horse.

If fluid is present in the stomach, the nature of the fluid can be helpful in determining the cause of the colic. Foul-smelling stomach fluid (not that any of it smells good) can be an indication of lack of intestinal movement. Stomach fluid that smells bad is also associated with inflammation of the intestines (this is known as enteritis). Dark fluid or fluid that looks like coffee grounds may indicate that bleeding has occurred in the stomach or upper small intestines.

Sometimes it is helpful to try to siphon stomach fluid by introducing a small amount of water into the tube first. Don't be surprised if your vet doesn't get any fluid back, however. In most horses with colic, fluid from the stomach cannot be obtained via a nasogastric tube.

· Figure 5 ·

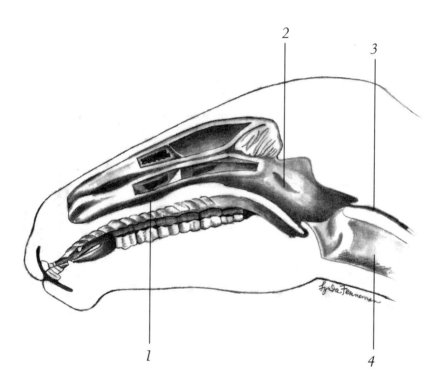

When a stomach tube is passed through the horse's nose, it goes through (1) the ventral nasal meatus; (2) the pharynx and (3) the narrow esophagus, on the way to the stomach. Make sure the tube isn't in the trachea (4) !

If a significant amount of fluid is obtained from the horse's stomach and the horse is considered a candidate for surgery, it's a good idea to send him to surgery with the nasogastric tube taped in place (to the halter). This can help prevent dangerous fluid accumulations that might occur while the horse is being transported to the hospital. While not all horses that accumulate fluid in their stomach have conditions that require surgery, all horses that are accumulating fluid need to have it relieved by a nasogastric tube.

BLOOD TESTS

Blood tests are generally not especially useful in the diagnosis of colic, particularly colics seen out in the field or on the farm. As previously noted, when a horse is initially evaluated for colic, a decision must be made rapidly as to whether the horse needs surgery. There is rarely time to perform or wait for extensive blood tests in a colicking horse, unless the horse is already at a facility that has laboratory equipment. Laboratory data usually does not help in deciding whether or not a horse with acute colic pain needs surgery.

Laboratory blood tests, however, can be useful in helping to decide the best way to medically support the horse prior to or after surgery. Some tests also appear to be useful in helping give a prognosis for recovery after surgery. The use of blood tests for these purposes is discussed in chapter seven.

Of course, blood tests may be very useful in helping to decide the cause of abdominal pain that is not related to acute disorders of the intestines. For example, disease of the liver or kidneys may be revealed by certain laboratory tests on the blood. Similarly, infectious conditions that may make the horse show colic-like pain can sometimes be detected with a blood test.

ABDOMINOCENTESIS (BELLY TAP)

The organs in the abdomen are bathed in a fluid known as the peritoneal (or abdominal) fluid. When it can be obtained (sometimes you just can't find any) from a colicking horse, an evaluation of it is easy, quick and sometimes very informative.

Abdominal fluid is obtained by sticking a needle or some other collecting device into the abdomen, along the midline of the horse's belly. Many horse owners are concerned that if a needle is stuck accidentally into the intestines, bad things will happen to the horse. In fact, accidental penetration of the bowel during abdominocentesis poses virtually no danger to the horse. The penetrated bowel seals itself very rapidly, and there is little, if any, leakage of intestinal contents through the puncture hole. To help reduce the possibility of contamination of the abdomen, however, the skin through which the needle is to be passed should be clipped and scrubbed with disinfectant solutions. The veterinarian doing the procedure should be wearing latex surgical gloves, as well.

The peritoneal fluid can change very quickly in horses with abdominal problems. Its composition is affected by infection and inflammation. The nature of the fluid depends to a great extent on what's going on inside the abdomen. Unfortunately, however, peritoneal fluid is not always helpful in making a diagnosis of the cause of a horse's colic. Sometimes severe conditions can exist inside the abdomen and the abdominal fluid will appear unaffected. For example, this could happen if an infection was contained and isolated by the horse's body, leaving the rest of the abdomen relatively unaffected.

Normal peritoneal fluid is clear and yellow or straw-colored. It does not form a clot because it is very low in protein. Peritoneal fluid will darken with abdominal bleeding or when blood pigment is released into the abdomen (such as happens with most intestinal twists). Protein levels of the fluid increase with both infection and inflammation in the abdomen.

Evaluation of cells found in the peritoneal fluid is also critical; certain types of cells may indicate abdominal infections, inflammation or tumors, for example. When cells are found in large numbers in the peritoneal fluid, the fluid becomes cloudy in appearance.

ABDOMINAL RADIOGRAPHS (X RAYS)

X rays of the abdomen can be particularly useful in detecting enteroliths (stones) and impactions of sand in the horse's intestines. On the X rays, sand and stones show up as large white areas in the abdomen. Radiographs are reportedly about 80 percent accurate in making a diagnosis of these conditions. Due to the power required for abdominal X rays, this must be done in a hospital.

ULTRASOUND

Ultrasound examinations of the abdomen are occasionally useful in making a diagnosis in the horse with colic. An ultrasound machine sends a sound wave into the horse's abdomen and picks up its echo; a computer interprets the echos and makes a grey-and-white image on the screen of the ultrasound machine. Ultrasound can be used to pick up gas accumulations or to detect areas of small intestinal distension. Ultrasound is also useful for looking at other areas of the horse's abdomen that may be diseased and associated with colic-like pain, such as the liver, spleen and kidneys.

THE DECISION FOR SURGERY

As mentioned earlier, the important things that need to be determined when your horse is being evaluated for colic are (1) whether the signs of colic are truly related to the intestines (generally, they are) and (2) whether the horse needs surgery. Your veterinarian will gather some or all of the aforementioned tests and try to formulate a clinical picture of your horse. With that information, he or she will try to determine how bad the problem truly is. Each individual test relates to the clinical signs that the horse is showing; no individual test is more important than another. If a number of tests indicate that the colic problem may be serious or the colic does not appear to be resolving over time, the index of suspicion that the horse may need surgery increases.

If your horse does need colic surgery or even if there is a suspicion that he does, get him to a hospital as quickly as possible. If the horse does need surgery, ideally he will be able to get it before too many adverse changes occur in his abdomen. If he does get surgery quickly, he will be more likely to come back home. If he doesn't need surgery, the worst thing that will happen is that your horse will have wasted your time and a trailer ride. Taking a horse to a veterinary hospital for observation of his colic is ultimately a very conservative decision; you are preparing for the worst-case circumstance and at the same time giving your horse the best chance for recovery. If you make a mistake in determining whether your horse needs surgery, make sure that the mistake you make is to take a horse that does not need surgery to the hospital. If you wait too long, your horse will not come home.

CHAPTER 5

Conditions Causing Colic or Colic-like Signs

Trying to categorize the various conditions that cause colics or colic-like pain is not easy (and perhaps not even wise). But when your veterinarian talks to you about a colic, he or she may try to describe to you the type of colic that your horse has. This chapter will try to characterize some of the most common conditions of the intestines that cause colic as well as some of the conditions that can be confused with intestinal problems.

It is not the goal of this book to try to describe in complete detail the causes, treatment and prognosis for each condition. The reader can find more information about each condition in standard veterinary texts, from your veterinarian or in other books in the Concise Guides series.

NONABDOMINAL CONDITIONS CAUSING COLIC-LIKE SIGNS

Laminitis

Laminitis is an incompletely understood inflammatory condition of the horse's feet. The laminae in the horse's feet are the connections between the live tissue on the inside of the foot and the dead hoof on the outside that covers the live tissue. Inflammation of these connecting laminae is called laminitis, also commonly referred to as founder. The causes of laminitis are many and include infections, diarrhea and excessive feeding. Laminitis can also occur as an unfortunate aftereffect of abdominal surgery.

Laminitis causes the feet of the horse to become very sore. Horses with laminitis are reluctant to walk because their feet hurt. Alternatively, they may walk stiffly or may be so sore that they do not want to get up and stand. This reluctance to move is occasionally confused with abdominal pain.

Laminitis is a medical condition that requires aggressive therapy and hoof care. Many horses do recover from laminitis. However, for other horses, it can be a devastating disease with disastrous consequences.

Pleuropneumonia (Pleuritis, Shipping Fever)

Pleuropneumonia is an infectious condition of the thoracic (chest) cavity of the horse. It is commonly seen after horses have been transported. Therefore, the name that is commonly used for the disease is shipping fever.

Horses with infections of their chest cavity generally eat poorly and can appear quite uncomfortable. Their respiration rate may be rapid or their breathing quite shallow. Sometimes, horses affected with this condition can be so uncomfortable or depressed that their condition can be confused with mild cases of colic. Unlike intestinal colics, however, most (but not all) horses with pleuropneumonia have a fever. A history of recent transport can also be important in distinguishing between the two conditions.

Pleuropneumonia requires a rapid and aggressive medical response with antibiotics and anti-inflammatory agents. Drainage of the infectious fluid from the chest is also usually required.

Exertional Rhabdomyolysis
(Tying-up, Azoturia, Myositis)

Exertional rhabdomyolysis is a condition of the horse's muscles. It is seen most commonly just after the onset of exercise. It can also be seen in horses that are exhausted, such as after endurance activity. However, acute onset myositis and myositis that occurs due to exhaustion are somewhat different in their causes and treatment.

Horses with rhabdomyolysis are usually very stiff and reluctant to move because of the muscle cramping that occurs as a result of the disease. This can be confused with the appearance of horses that are experiencing colic pain. The history of vigorous exercise preceding the pain and stiffness is usually a valuable tool in differentiating between the two conditions.

COLIC-LIKE CONDITIONS CAUSED BY
ABDOMINAL INFECTION OR INFLAMMATION

Abdominal Abscesses

Bacterial abscesses of the abdominal lymph nodes occur occasionally in the horse. They are most commonly seen after outbreaks of streptococcal bacterial infections (strangles) in horses. However, other things can cause abdominal abscesses, too. For example, some people believe that horses that are heavily parasitized are at increased risk for the development of abdominal abscesses. This is because as parasites migrate through the abdomen as part of their life cycle, there may be secondary contamination by bacteria. Horses with an abdominal abscess usually have a fever, do not eat and may show signs of colic-like pain.

Abdominal abscesses usually respond to long-term antibiotic therapy. However, surgery has been described for some conditions where the abscess blocks the intestines. The prognosis for recovery is generally good if a quick response is made to antibiotics; complications such as intestinal adhesions (scarring) and abscess rupture are associated with a much poorer outcome.

Peritonitis

Peritonitis is inflammation of the abdominal cavity. It can occur because of infection or chemical irritation (such as with a ruptured bladder in a foal with urine leakage into the abdomen). Infections of the abdomen can come from a number of causes, including intestinal perforations, internal abscesses, rectal tears, postbreeding vaginal tears and postsurgery.

In addition to colic-like pain, most horses with peritonitis have a fever. Abdominocentesis usually is diagnostic for the problem. Blood tests can also be helpful in determining the severity of the body's response to the infections and/or inflammation.

Horses with peritonitis are generally treated with antibiotics and anti-inflammatory drugs. Surgery may be required for some conditions associated with peritonitis, such as a ruptured bladder. Surgical drainage of the inflamed abdomen has also been advocated in some cases of peritonitis, although this treatment has its own problems. The prognosis for resolution of peritonitis is guarded (keep your fingers crossed) to grave (not likely to make it), especially if there has been rupture of the intestines with fecal contamination inside the abdomen.

Colitis

Colitis is a serious inflammatory condition of the large bowel. Its most obvious sign is a severe, profuse diarrhea. There are many factors involved with the onset of colitis, including bacterial infection and severe metabolic stress. Unfortunately, such things can often occur after surgery.

Colitis is a very difficult condition to treat in the horse. In colitis, huge amounts of fluid may be lost by the horse in the feces. Treatment of colitis is made even more difficult by a variety of metabolic complications that can occur with the disease, including shock, endotoxemia (absorption of bacterial endotoxin; endotoxin is a component part of certain intestinal bacteria) and laminitis.

Aggressive medical therapy is indicated in colitis cases, usually including huge amounts of intravenous fluids (25 gallons or more per day). The prognosis for recovery from colitis is generally guarded to poor and much worse if additional metabolic complications occur.

Potomac Horse Fever

Potomac horse fever (Equine Monocytic Ehrlichiosis) is caused by a bloodborne microorganism that is neither a virus nor a bacteria. The infectious agent is called a rickettsia. The exact mode of transmission of Potomac horse fever is not known. However, it is not considered to be a contagious disease that is spread by direct horse-to-horse contact or from contamination of the environment. An insect such as a tick is suspected to be the vector for transmission of the disease. Unfortunately, the method of transmission has yet to be proven.

Clinical signs of Potomac horse fever can vary greatly between horses but include fever, depression, diarrhea, laminitis and colic. Horses with Potomac horse fever can look a lot like horses with colitis. Aggressive medical therapy with intravenous fluids and tetracycline antibiotics is mandatory in severe cases; some horses die in spite of aggressive therapy.

A vaccination is available to aid in the prevention of Potomac horse fever. The vaccine provides an approximately 80 percent protection rate in experimental situations of infection.

Proximal Enteritis (Duodenitis-Jejunitis)

Proximal enteritis is a disease of the anterior segments of the small intestine. Its cause is unknown. Proximal enteritis is seen more commonly in the southeast and northeast United States than in other parts of the country.

Proximal enteritis causes fever, depression and mild to severe colic-like signs. Laminitis can also be a complication of this disease. In addition, large amounts of gastric and intestinal fluid may reflux back through the horse's nose or via a stomach tube when a horse is affected with this disease.

Treatment is medical. Continuous decompression of the stomach and its contents with a nasogastric tube is important to prevent stomach rupture. Fluid therapy, antibiotics and nonsteroidal anti-inflammatory drugs are also used in treatment. Unfortunately, even with aggressive medical therapy, proximal enteritis is a life-ending condition for many horses.

Clinically, proximal enteritis may be easily confused with surgical colic conditions that cause obstruction and dilation of the small intestines. Both small intestinal obstructions and proximal enteritis cause the intestines to become dilated with excessive fluid; both conditions cause signs of colic; both conditions can be associated with large volumes of fluid coming back up from the stomach. Because of the difficulty of distinguishing between the two conditions, horses with proximal enteritis sometimes are operated on due to their clinical signs. Fortunately, surgery does not pose an undue risk to these horses. Occasionally a clinical judgment call must be made by the veterinarian and a risk taken by the owner if it is not possible to tell the difference between the two conditions. Without surgery, horses with small intestinal obstructions may die; with surgery, horses affected with proximal enteritis can still recover.

Colic-like Problems
Associated with Abdominal Organs
Uterine Torsion

Torsion of the uterus is a rare condition seen in mares late in pregnancy. A torsion is a twist, like the twist put in some loaves of bread. The mare's uterus twists on itself and causes disruption of the blood supply to the uterus. This causes tissue death and severe colic-like pain for the poor mare that has the problem.

Correction of uterine torsion is usually done surgically, although rolling the mare has been suggested as a way to try to correct the twist. The prognosis for the mare and foal depends on how badly the uterus was twisted and how long it was twisted before the twist was corrected.

Liver and Biliary Problems

A number of liver problems can be associated with colic-like signs in the horse, particularly if the liver dysfunction causes problems with normal intestinal movement. Most liver problems show up slowly, over time. They cause horses to waste away or be unthrifty. However, chronic conditions that occur over time can become acute and an immediate problem if the liver finally becomes overwhelmed by the chronic disease process. Liver problems potentially associated with colic include infection, cancer, plant toxicities and cirrhosis (chronic liver scarring).

The prognosis for recovery from most chronic liver conditions is guarded to poor, even with proper dietary and medical management. (Acute conditions of the liver, such as some infections, are also seen in the horse. The signs associated with acute liver infections rarely include colic.)

The biliary system collects the fluid produced by the liver (known as the bile) and expels it into the duodenum of the small intestine via the bile duct. Just like everything else in the horse, the bile duct can have problems, too. It can become obstructed with small stones (these are called choleliths) in the same way that the intestines can become obstructed by enteroliths. The reason these stones form in the biliary system is not known. They are much more common in older horses, although horses as young as one year of age have been reported to have biliary stones.

The treatment for biliary stones is surgical removal. The prognosis for recovery is good if there has not been extensive secondary liver damage.

Bladder Problems

Problems with the bladder of the horse are not particularly common. The most frequently encountered conditions are ruptured bladders in newborn foals and bladder stones in adult horses, especially males. When present, these conditions can be associated with straining and colic-like signs.

Both ruptured bladder and bladder stones are conditions that require surgical correction. Both conditions are generally associated with a good prognosis after surgery.

Kidney Problems

Rarely, acute or chronic failure of the horse's kidneys can cause colic-like signs. More commonly, kidney disease in the horse is associated with weight loss and lack of appetite.

Neoplastic Conditions (Cancer) That Cause Colic or Colic-like Signs

Cancer of any sort is uncommon in horses. However, a number of types of cancer can cause colic-like signs. Among the more frequently seen types of cancer in the horse are:

- Lymphosarcoma, a cancer of the horse's lymphatic system. (The lymphatic system is a system of small vessels that carry fluid derived from tissue throughout the body.) Lymphosarcoma can occur in horses of any age but is more common in older horses. Several different forms of lymphosarcoma have been described in the horse.

- Lipoma, a tumor of the body's fat. Lipomas tend to originate from fat that is deposited in the mesentery, the supporting tissue of the intestines.

    Lipomas can be especially serious for a horse. The tumors tend to grow from the mesentery as a stalk of tissue. The lipomas themselves don't cause the horse any trouble. The stalk of the tumor, however, can wrap around a segment of intestines like a tight band and strangulate the blood supply. A strangulating lipoma is a condition that needs to be recognized and corrected quickly at surgery. It is seen almost exclusively in horses older than twelve years of age.

- Squamous cell carcinoma, most commonly seen in the horse's stomach. This is a condition that occurs more commonly in middle-aged to older horses than in younger horses. It is seen in male horses more than in females. Unfortunately, the clinical signs of stomach cancer in the horse are vague and come on slowly. Once these tumors have been discovered, it is usually too late to treat the horse.

- Leiomyoma or leiomyosarcoma, tumors of the muscles of the intestines. These tumors can sometimes obstruct the intestines. Successful surgery to remove these tumors has been described. They rarely, if ever, spread to other sites in the body.

INTESTINAL PROBLEMS THAT CAUSE COLIC

Spasmodic Colic

Spasmodic colic is a condition that cannot really be proven in the horse. It seems logical that it should sometimes happen, though. A spasm refers to a sudden, rapid, involuntary and uncoordinated contraction of muscles. In the case of the colicking horse, the muscles that are thought to spasm are those of the intestinal wall, the muscles that cause the movement of the intestines. Muscular contraction and spasm of the bowel could cause pain, interfere with normal intestinal function and temporarily constrict the intestinal canal.

You can't prove that there really was a spasm in the middle of 100 feet of intestines that made the horse colic. Therefore, the term "spasmodic colic" is generally used to try to explain a colic for which there is no other obvious reason or cause. Such inexplicable colics are seen frequently in the horse. They almost invariably resolve themselves with or without treatment. Understandably, spasmodic colics do cause a lot of anxiety in horses as well as in their owners.

Verminous Arteritis (Worms)

Strongylus vulgaris is one of the internal parasites of the horse. Part of its complex life cycle includes migration of parasitic larvae in the branches of the main artery that supplies the large intestines, the cranial mesenteric artery.

When parasitic larvae occur in large numbers in the artery, they can cause the horse lots of problems. The mere presence of the larvae in the artery can cause colic pain. Colic may also be caused be the migration of the larvae from the artery into the intestines (just prior to their reaching the adult stage).

The most serious health problem for the horse associated with parasitic larvae is thought to be caused by the production of blood clots (thrombi). The presence of the larvae in the artery causes roughening of the internal surface of that vessel. This disrupts the normal smooth flow of blood. The turbulence and roughening inside the vessel allows for blood clots to form. These clots can then break loose and travel in the horse's bloodstream (the clots are then called emboli); the term *thromboembolic colic* is sometimes used to describe this problem. Eventually, these clots can lodge in small blood vessels and block circulation to the tissue supplied by them (this situation is called an infarction).

Blockage of the blood vessels and the resultant loss of circulation to the intestine can cause death of the affected segment of the intestinal tract. Verminous arteritis is a very serious condition that has, at best, a guarded prognosis for recovery, even with surgery.

Impaction

An impaction is an accumulation of feed or other material in the intestines. Impactions are most commonly seen in the large intestines, but they can occur anywhere in the intestinal tract. Impacted material can block the passage of feed through the intestines.

Other problems can occur behind an intestinal obstruction (just as problems can occur behind an accident on the freeway). Behind the impaction, the bowel can dilate with fluid and/or gas. This causes the colic pain. If an impaction persists, the normal mixing movements of the intestines can squeeze water out of the impacted mass. This causes the mass to become drier and firmer and makes the problem worse.

Certain types of impactions are more common in individual animals. Newborn foals may have an impaction of the meconium (meconium is the first manure, which is formed from a mixture of intestinal secretions and the fetal fluid). In an effort to prevent meconium impactions, many foals are given an enema within 24 hours of the time that they hit the ground, whether they need it or not. Impactions of the cecum are generally seen in older horses. Such things as poor dental care and water deprivation or lack of drinking have also been suggested as causes of impaction.

Impactions usually respond to medical efforts to moisten and dislodge them from the intestines. The clinical signs of this type of colic are generally mild. Most impactions have a good prognosis for recovery. Even so, some impactions require surgery to relieve them; the prognosis for these colics is also good if surgery is initiated before any severe metabolic complications occur.

Ulcers

Ulcers are, by definition, defects in the surface of any membrane, tissue or organ. In the horse, ulcers are generally seen in the stomach. Stomach ulcers occur more commonly in foals but are also seen in adult horses. The factors that cause stomach ulcers in foals are not known but they are thought to include stress and rapid growth. Horses with ulcers may show signs of colic, be unthrifty and lose weight. Ulcers in the horse's stomach can be very difficult to diagnose unless a special three-yard-long gastro-scope is used to look around in the horse's stomach.

Treatment of stomach ulcers usually is medical. However, surgeries have been performed in serious cases of ulcers that ruptured through the stomach. The response to medical treatment of ulcers is generally good; the response to surgery is somewhat less so.

Rectal Tears

Tearing of the rectum is most frequently seen as a complication of a routine rectal examination. However, it can be seen in some horses as a spontaneous occurrence, with no apparent cause. Following rectal exam, a tear should be suspected if there is a large amount of fresh blood on the rectal sleeve of the person who did the examination or if there is fresh blood coming from the rectum. Rectal examinations should never be performed by people who do not have training in doing them.

A horse with a suspected rectal tear should be hospitalized immedi-ately. He is a potential candidate for surgery. Depending on the severity of the tear and whether there has been fecal contamination into the ab-domen, the prognosis for recovery from a rectal tear can be good to poor.

Gas Colic

The horse's large intestine ferments the horse's feed. Of course, this feed has already been digested once by the stomach and small intestine. Fermentation allows the horse to obtain nutrients from relatively non-nutritious substances such as hay, substances that humans can't even eat.

Gas is a by-product of fermentation (that's why beer bubbles). Large amounts of gas can accumulate in the horse's large intestine when the hay or pasture is particularly green and rich. It can also build up if there is interference with the normal passage of feed material through the bowel.

High-grain diets are also associated with gas colics. Gas buildup causes the intestines to stretch; stretching of the intestines causes pain; pain makes horses colic.

Gas colic is generally relieved medically. The prognosis for full recovery is usually quite good.

Large Colon Displacements

The large colon of the horse occupies the majority of the horse's lower abdomen. Because it can move around, the large intestine can become displaced from its normal position in the abdomen. Displacements are reportedly more common in large, warmblood breeds than in other types of horses.

Why things get so mixed up in the abdomen is anyone's guess. However, abnormal propulsive movements of the intestine (which are impossible to prove) have been suggested as the cause. Trying to describe where the colon segments move to can get a bit confusing; it will help you to understand the abnormal positions that the colon finds itself in if you look back at the anatomy drawings in chapter 2. The most commonly seen colon displacements in the horse are these:

- Displacement of the left colons over the top of the spleen in the renosplenic space (there is a space between the top of the spleen and the left kidney). This type of displacement is also called a nephrosplenic entrapment. In this type of colic, the left dorsal and ventral colons can either sneak up between the spleen and the left body wall or they can somehow negotiate the space that normally exists between the stomach and the spleen. Either way, part of the left colon becomes "trapped" by the spleen and the passage of feed through the area becomes impeded or stopped. Sometimes this condition can be diagnosed by rectal examination.

The treatment for nephrosplenic entrapment of the left colons is generally surgical. Some horses, however, have had their problem corrected under general anesthesia by being rolled around. The prognosis for recovery is good, especially with early surgical intervention.

- Displacement of the left colons to the right of the cecum. This condition is called a right dorsal displacement. In this condition, the left dorsal and ventral colons get displaced between the cecum and the body wall. There are actually several different variations in the way that the colons can get twisted up in right dorsal displacement. These things have to be sorted out and corrected during surgery.

  Unlike left dorsal displacements, right dorsal colon displacements cannot be corrected by rolling the horse. Again, assuming early surgical intervention, prior to secondary metabolic complications or tissue death, the prognosis for recovery is good.

- Displacement of the pelvic flexure and/or left colons. Since the left colons of the horse are very mobile, they can get into a lot of trouble. When the pelvic flexure gets displaced, it usually tends to end up in the front of the abdomen, up by the sternum. This type of displacement usually doesn't twist the bowel, but it can hamper the flow of feed through the gut.

  Unfortunately, the pelvic flexure can also get trapped in various places in the abdomen. Entrapment of the pelvic flexure in tears of the ligament that runs between the stomach and the spleen are sometimes seen. Entrapment through hernias in the diaphragm also occurs occasionally. (Diaphragmatic hernias most commonly occur in mares after foaling. Apparently, the mares strain so hard during birth that they rip a hole in their diaphragm. The colon then moves right on into the chest!)

Like other colon displacements, correction of pelvic flexure problems requires surgery. The prognosis for recovery is usually good.

Intestinal Twists (Torsion of the Large Colon and Volvulus of the Small Intestine)

Twists of the intestines are very serious conditions. They cause severe colic signs in the horse. When twists occur, the blood supply to the intestines is reduced or stopped; tissue death of the intestines begins. These conditions must be recognized and treated wtih surgery very quickly in order for the outcome to be successful.

A volvulus describes the twisting of the small intestine on its supporting mesentery. To illustrate this problem, imagine that you are holding a marionette, a puppet that is moved by supporting strings. In this example, the puppet is the intestine and the strings that move the arms and legs are the mesentery, through which run the blood vessels that supply the intestine. If you were to spin the puppet so that its strings twisted, this would be analogous to what happens during volvulus of the small intestine. Large loops of small intestine can become involved in a small intestinal volvulus. These twists can incorporate and compromise 30 or 40 feet of the bowel!

Volvulus of the small intestine must be recognized and corrected immediately. If death of some portion of the small intestine has occurred, that segment must be removed. There is a limit, however, to how much of the small intestine can be removed. Sometimes, unfortunately, the sheer amount of dying intestines in the horse means that a successful surgery will not be possible.

A torsion is a twisting of the large colon upon itself. To picture this problem, imagine that you have in your hand a long balloon, the kind used to make balloon animals. Hold one end of the balloon firmly in one hand. With your other hand, twist the other end of the balloon. The twist that occurs in the balloon mimics what happens with large intestinal torsion.

Torsions are described by the amount of rotation that occurs. The more the intestine rotates, the more complete the interruption of the blood supply and the more serious the situation is for the horse.

Torsions are described by the degree of their rotation. To explain the degree of rotation, think again of the balloon. This time, mark the end of the balloon that you are twisting with a felt marker. When the end of the balloon is twisted so that the mark returns to where it began, this would be a twist of 360 degrees (there are 360 degrees in a circle). Lesser torsions of 180 and 270 degrees and greater torsions of up to 720 degrees (twice around the circle) have all been seen in the horse.

Large colon torsions are seen most commonly in older horses, in mares and especially in mares that are late in their pregnancies. Both a mare and the foal she is carrying can survive surgery for colon torsion if the surgery is begun quickly enough. Horses with severe colon torsions can deteriorate very quickly, however. Every moment is critical when it comes to getting them to surgery.

Hernias and Incarcerations

A hernia of the intestines is the protrusion of a loop of intestine through an abnormal opening. The intestine is said to be incarcerated when it is entrapped in any opening, abnormal or otherwise. When the intestine herniates or becomes incarcerated, the loop of intestine that goes through the opening gets trapped and loses its blood supply. It's as if a rubber band had been put around the loop of affected intestines. The loop of bowel trapped in the tissue opening will then begin to die. Obviously, this is a situation that needs to be recognized quickly and corrected surgically. From a practical standpoint, the result of an incarceration or a herniation is the same thing.

Interestingly, as serious as these conditions are, the clinical signs associated with hernias and incarcerations are sometimes vague and confusing. Frequently, these colics are remarkable not so much for the intensity of the pain that is demonstrated by the horse as for the fact that the pain just won't go away. Sometimes the nature of the pain with these types of colic is relatively mild, even if the condition is relatively serious. Because of this, sometimes the hernias and incarcerations are not recognized until after serious metabolic changes and tissue death have occurred.

Herniations and incarcerations seen in the horse include:

- Inguinal hernias in stallions. In this case, a loop of small intestine goes through the inguinal canal and ends up in the scrotum of the stallion. Inguinal hernias can also be seen in newborn foals. These hernias usually are treated by castration and surgical closure of the inguinal canal.
- Diaphragmatic hernias. These are most commonly seen in mares after foaling. It is thought that straining during foaling causes the diaphragm to rip; intestines, especially the left colons, can go through the hole and herniate into the chest cavity.
- Umbilical hernias. When foals are born, occasionally a defect in the body wall will remain where the umbilical cord originated. It is possible for intestines to become herniated and trapped through these holes in the abdominal wall.
- Epiploic foramen herniations. It is virtually impossible to describe what the epiploic foramen is to someone who does not have a detailed knowledge of the anatomy of the horse's abdomen. A foramen is a natural opening or passage; the epiploic foramen is a very small, flat opening that exists just behind the liver, in the top of the abdomen. There is no apparent reason for its being there.

Small intestine (especially the jejunum) can go through the epiploic foramen and become incarcerated. These colics can be especially difficult to recognize. They always require surgical correction. For surgery to be successful, it needs to be done early.

- Incarceration of intestines through a variety of tears in the mesentery and various internal ligaments of the abdomen, such as the gastrosplenic ligament, the cecocolic ligament and the renosplenic ligament. These conditions are mostly distinguished from each other by the tissue through which the bowel gets entrapped. In the field, during the examination, it's impossible (and not important) to tell them apart.

Intussusception

An intussusception describes a situation in which one piece of intestine is entrapped within another, much as the segments of a telescope fold into each other. This is not a particularly common condition. For some reason it is seen almost exclusively in horses of three years of age or less. Intussusceptions of the small intestine, of the ileum into the cecum, of the colon into the cecum and of the large colon have all been seen. Large colon intussusceptions in adult horses have been associated with the presence of tapeworms in the intestine.

The treatment for intussusception is surgery. The prognosis for recovery is good, assuming that surgery is initiated prior to the onset of adverse metabolic changes.

Enteroliths (Stones)

Enteroliths, or stones, can develop in the large intestine over a period of time. They form much as a pearl forms in an oyster. Layers of mineral are deposited on each other over time, usually around some little irritant such as a piece of wire or a bottle cap.

In some cases, horses will pass small stones before they become a problem. Such stones generally look like flat, gray rocks in the manure. In other cases, however, the stones can become large enough to obstruct the intestines. Some stones may be as large as a basketball! In these cases, surgical removal is required. The prognosis with surgery is usually very good unless the horse gets to surgery very late in the course of his colic.

Because enteroliths take time to form, they are rarely if ever seen in horses less than four years old. They are reported more frequently in Arabian horses and in horses living in Florida, California and Indiana. Some people have tried to connect the occurrence of intestinal stones with high mineral content in the horse's water, although there is no clear evidence of such an association. Others have tried to implicate the feeding of wheat bran; again, there's no proof of that causing problems with enteroliths.

Sand Colic

Horses that live in environments that have large amounts of sand are prone to sand colic. In these areas, horses that are fed on the ground or that vacuum every square inch of terrain looking for that last leaf of hay are likely to consume sand with each mouthful of feed. The sand can accumulate in the intestines.

Sand is also irritating to the intestines of the horse. The presence of sand in the bowel can cause the intestines to secrete water. For that reason, the early signs of sand colic often include diarrhea.

If sand accumulates in the intestines, however, it can cause a complete obstruction of the bowel. The signs of colic can be severe in these horses. Smaller amounts of sand can be removed by treatment with psyllium (see chapter 6). However, it can be difficult or impossible to remove large amounts of sand from the bowel with medical treatment alone.

At surgery, impactions of sand weighing seventy pounds or more have been seen!

Now that you've read abut the types of colic, it's time to learn what you can do about them.

CHAPTER 6

Medical Management of the Colicking Horse

Horses with acute disease of the abdomen need prompt medical treatment. If your veterinarian has decided that the horse with signs of colic should be managed medically (that is, he does not need surgery or needs to be stabilized prior to surgery), the treatment is obviously aimed at correcting the perceived problem(s). Fortunately, most colics are relatively mild. These types of colics frequently get described as "spasmodic" or "gas" or "verminous" colics. Happily, these horses will almost invariably get better.

Many different treatments are used in the medical treatment of colics. Basically, however, treatment for these conditions involves just two things: control of the pain and return of the function of the intestines to normal. After therapy is given to a horse, the horse should be monitored carefully for the period of time indicated by your veterinarian, to make sure that the therapy did what it was supposed to. If, after the initial therapy is given, the horse does not get better, he must be re-evaluated.

Additional therapeutic measures, possibly even surgery, may be required if the colic does not resolve.

CONTROL OF PAIN

Colic pain can be some of the most severe pain experienced by the horse. Control of the pain is a cornerstone of colic therapy. Pain control is important for many reasons, not the least of which are humane.

Horses that are experiencing colic pain may thrash and roll around. These poor horses are just trying to get comfortable. They do this with no regard for their safety or surroundings. As a result, they can scrape themselves up, get caught in the corner of a stall (cast themselves) or otherwise damage their head, legs and body. Pain control can therefore help prevent the horse from hurting himself. (Remember, horses do not twist their intestines by rolling around.) Pain control can also help prevent the horse from hurting the people around him who are trying to handle him. (It can help relieve the people's concern and distress, as well.)

Pain itself also has a negative effect on the movement of the intestines. Pain stops intestinal movement. Relief of pain can help stop spasm of the bowel.

Pain control must not be done indiscriminately, however. You don't just want to continually cover up a real problem. The clinical signs of colic pain are important to recognize. If colic pain disappears, the colic problem usually has been resolved. If pain persists, it suggests a more serious condition. The type and degree of pain is one of the things used to decide whether a horse needs surgery. Continued masking of pain with drugs that relieve pain can allow a horse's surgical colic to progress to the point where surgical intervention may come too late.

Four groups of pharmacologic agents may be selected by your veterinarian for pain control in the colicking horse.

Nonsteroidal Anti-inflammatory Drugs

The most commonly used nonsteroidal anti-inflammatory drugs used in the horse for the control of colic pain are dipyrone, phenylbutazone (bute) and flunixin meglumine (Banamine). These drugs all come from the same chemical family. They all control pain in the same manner, by interfering with the production of a chemical that is associated with the sensation of pain. Experimentally, these drugs differ greatly in their ability to control colic pain, however.

Dipyrone is a very weak analgesic drug. If and when it works, it provides only short-term relief of very mild abdominal pain. On the plus side, dipyrone is very safe. Several doses can be given over a period of a few hours, when desired. Some veterinarians, however, feel that dipyrone is completely ineffective for relief of colic pain.

Phenylbutazone (bute) has been demonstrated to be no more effective than dipyrone in controlling colic pain in the horse. It also has some disadvantages over dipyrone in that it cannot be given by injection into the muscle. Also, there is not a wide margin of safety with phenylbutazone. Side effects have occasionally been associated with long-term use of this drug, although this really doesn't become a problem in the short term. It is extremely unlikely that any adverse effects in the horse would be seen if the recommended dose of phenylbutazone were exceeded over a 24- to 48-hour period.

Flunixin meglumine (Banamine) has been demonstrated to be the most effective nonsteroidal anti-inflammatory drug available for the control of colic pain. The duration of pain relief obtained from a single injection of flunixin is quite variable. Pain relief may last from 1 to 24 hours, depending on the cause and the intensity of the pain.

Some veterinarians feel that flunixin can mask signs of colic pain. They believe that flunixin is such a potent pain reliever that it may make it harder to recognize that surgical intervention is required. However, experimental data indicates that flunixin is not an extremely potent pain-relieving drug. The feeling held by some veterinarians that flunixin should never be used in horses with colic pain is therefore difficult to understand. However, if a horse continues to show pain after pain-relieving drugs such as flunixin have been administered, it is absolutely mandatory that he be re-evaluated to make sure that the colic problem is not worse than what was originally thought.

Sedative-Analgesic Drugs

Xylazine (Rompun) and detomodine (Dormosedan) are two sedatives that decrease the horse's awareness of the painful stimuli associated with colic. These two drugs are also chemically related, although xylazine is a shorter-acting drug than detomodine. Both drugs are extremely effective at controlling colic pain, much more so than the nonsteroidal anti-inflammatory drugs. The sedation that is caused by these drugs can also be useful in assisting in rectal examination and nasogastric intubation of the affected horses.

Both xylazine and detomodine can usually mask even the most severe colic pain. If, however, colic pain returns a few minutes after a colicking horse has been given these drugs, it suggests that the horse's problem may require surgical intervention. Especially with these potent pain-relieving drugs, indiscriminate and continuous masking of colic pain in the horse should not be done. These drugs can prevent the recognition of a serious problem until it's too late.

Opioid Analgesic Drugs

Pure narcotic drugs, like morphine, are potent relievers of pain in people. They are not widely used in the horse for a number of reasons. Narcotics can stop intestinal movement, which is not desirable in the colicking horse. In addition, narcotics cause many horses to become extremely agitated and excited.

Two narcotic derivatives are occasionally used in the horse for control of colic pain. Butorphanol (Torbugesic) gives the best pain relief with the fewest side effects. It may also be combined with xylazine to increase the pain-relieving effect. On the other hand, pentazocine (Talwin-V) appears to be a much weaker drug than butorphanol. Pentazocine is controlled by the U.S. Food and Drug Administration because it is a potentially addictive drug that can be abused by people. For this reason, many veterinarians don't like to have pentazocine around so people won't be tempted to steal it.

WALKING OR EXERCISING THE HORSE

Walking the horse is one of the things almost everyone recommends to help "treat" the pain of a colicking horse. There seem to be a number of reasons for this. While some of the reasons don't make much sense, at least walking the horse is something that usually doesn't make the situation any worse. It also keeps everyone around the colicking horse busy until the veterinarian gets on the scene.

Walking or exercising the colicking horse may even be mildly beneficial in relieving colic pain. It's not at all clear why this is so, but some horses do seem to get some relief from their colic pain just by moving around. A ride in a horse trailer can have a similar effect; sometimes when a horse is sent off to surgery in a trailer, he arrives at the hospital with his head up and ready to eat (his only danger at that time is from a frustrated owner).

Walking or exercising the horse does not help prevent twisting of the intestines. The most critical and potentially life-threatening colics are those that involve twisting or entrapment of the intestines; these are also the most painful colics. *Horses with twisted intestines roll around because they hurt so much; rolling around does not twist their intestines.* The painful twist comes before the rolling. If rolling around caused intestinal twists, you'd think that you'd see lots of twists after horses rolled around normally. Have you ever seen or heard of a horse that ended up with a twist in his intestines after being allowed to go out and roll around in a pasture or in an arena?

Nor does walking or exercise prevent death of the horse. Some people fear that if a horse lies down he might die. If the horse does eventually die from his colic, he's going to lie down.

CORRECTION OF FLUID DEFECITS

Many horses with colic problems will refuse to drink water. Alternatively, colicking horses may be in some form of metabolic crisis, such as shock, in which the horse's body is trying its best to maintain circulation to the most critical areas, such as the heart and brain. In either case, when treating the horse with colic, it is very important to make sure that the horse is adequately hydrated. In other words, make sure he has enough water in his system in order to help prevent further metabolic complications.

Fluids can be provided to the horse either orally, via nasogastric intubation (stomach tube) or intravenously. The oral or nasogastric route of giving fluids is somewhat easier to administer, but its effectiveness is also more limited; the intestines may not absorb water well if their function is already being compromised by colic. In addition, the size of the stomach limits the amount of fluids that can be given orally.

Consequently, intravenous fluids are recommended for the treatment of some cases of colic. In some conditions, such as colic caused by infectious diarrhea, fluid therapy must be very aggressive. Horses with diarrhea can lose as much as 100 liters (more than 25 gallons) of fluid per day. Indeed, one of the real problems with treatment of infectious diarrheas is that it is very difficult to keep up with this volume of fluid loss by the horse.

In other cases, such as those horses with dried or impacted feces in the intestines or in cases of sand colic, fluid therapy is used in an effort to get water into the impacted mass of material. Horses may be slightly hyper-hydrated with intravenous fluids (given more fluid than their body really needs) in hopes that fluid will leak into the intestines. This might moisten the fecal material and make its movement easier. This sort of therapy is sometimes accompanied by the oral administration of laxative salts such as magnesium sulfate (epsom salts). Laxative salts tend to draw extra water given IV into the intestines by an osmotic effect.

In horses in early stages of shock, administration of hypertonic solutions has been advocated by some veterinarians. Body fluids contain salts; most intravenous solutions generally contain salts in a similar proportion to that contained in the body fluids (those fluids are isotonic). Hypertonic solutions are those that contain higher amounts of salts than the body fluids. Hypertonic solutions can draw water from the body into the circulatory system to help maintain the volume of fluid in the blood vessels. In the short term, maintaining the horse's circulation by giving him hypertonic solutions may help keep his circulatory system from collapsing. This may be very important when time is of the essence, say, while trying to stabilize a horse that is about to be transported to the hospital for surgery. In such cases, there may be no time to administer large volumes of isotonic (normal salt concentration) fluids.

LUBRICANTS, LAXATIVES AND CATHARTICS

Horses with suspected medical colics are sometimes given substances via nasogastric intubation (stomach tube) as part of their treatment. These substances try to restore normal intestinal movement in a number of ways: by bringing water into the bowel, by stimulating bowel movement or by softening the mass of material in the intestines. Those effects are called laxative.

Horses that have significant reflux of stomach contents back through a stomach tube should not be given any additional type of fluid through the tube. Loading additional fluid into a system that may already be plugged up is not beneficial. Additional fluid in an obstructed and overloaded system can cause it to rupture.

Laxative agents attempt to increase the water content in the mass of fecal material. This helps soften the feces and move it through the intestines. Green grass and alfalfa hay can have a laxative effect, although no one knows why. Four different laxative agents are commonly employed for the treatment of colic.

Mineral Oil

Light mineral oil is probably the most commonly used laxative in horses. How and why mineral oil works is not well understood. It seems most likely that a coating of mineral oil inside the intestines interferes with the absorption of water by the intestines (oil and water don't mix). If mineral oil causes water to be poorly absorbed by the intestines, the amount of water within the bowel may therefore be indirectly increased. There may be some lubricating effect from mineral oil as well. Mineral oil does not penetrate the feces, however.

One of the nice things about mineral oil is that the owner and veterinarian can see when it passes through the horse (it makes an obvious mess on the rear of the horse). This can be an indication that the horse's colic is over. Unfortunately, however, mineral oil can also pass around some impactions without relieving them.

Dioctyl Sodium Sulfosuccinate (DSS)

DSS is a stimulant laxative. DSS is mixed with water prior to being given to colicking horses. It irritates the intestinal wall and makes the intestinal muscles contract. DSS is also a surface tension-reducing agent.

Surface tension describes a physical condition that preserves the integrity of a surface. For example, there is a point at which the water in a glass actually can exceed the rim without the water spilling over the sides. This is because of its surface tension. By reducing the surface tension of gas bubbles or ingested feed, DSS allows water to penetrate, causing softening of the fecal mass or reduction in the size of the gas bubbles.

DSS also increases fluid and electrolyte secretion by the cells of the intestinal wall. This further increases the amount of water in the bowel and helps to soften the feces.

It is generally recommended that DSS not be given along with mineral oil. Theoretically, by reducing the surface tension of the mineral oil, DSS could cause the mineral oil to be broken down into small enough globules to be absorbed into the circulation. Clinically, this hasn't been seen to be a problem. If it occurred, however, it would certainly be harmful to the horse's system.

Overdoses of DSS can make horses sick. Therefore, it is recommended that if additional doses of DSS are required, they be given at 48-hour intervals.

Psyllium Hydrophillic Mucilloid

Psyllium is a bulk laxative. It is a powderlike substance that comes from seeds of the psyllium plant.

Psyllium absorbs water in large amounts (hence the term *hydrophyllic* from the Greek roots *hydro* for water and *phyl* for to love). When it does so, it turns into a gooey mess (mucilloid). Because it absorbs so much water and keeps the water in the intestines, psyllium can be an effective agent for softening impacted masses of feed.

Psyllium is particularly useful for removing masses of sand from the intestines. It can be given by nasogastric intubation. Psyllium is also available in many over-the-counter formulations designed to prevent the accumulation of sand.

Psyllium should not be given continuously to horses. Psyllium is not dangerous but if it is fed continuously, the bacteria of the horse's intestines could begin to digest it. This decreases its effectiveness. Therefore, to maintain its effectiveness, if psyllium is used to help prevent sand accumulations, some authorities recommend daily dosing for 3 weeks every 4 to 6 months.

Magnesium Sulfate (Epsom Salts)

Magnesium sulfate is an osmotic laxative. When high concentrations of salts are put into the intestines, water is drawn to them (this process is called osmosis). Thus, administration of epsom salts via a nasogastric tube is one method used to try to increase the water content in the intestines. In an effort to help increase this effect, magnesium sulfate is also frequently given in conjunction with intravenous fluids. The hope here is that the additional fluids that are being pumped into the horse's veins will be drawn into the intestines by the high salt content.

Magnesium sulfate must always be given in water. If it is not diluted, it can cause inflammation of the intestines. Authorities recommend that magnesium sulfate not be given for more than three consecutive days, in order to avoid problems with intestinal irritation as well as problems from magnesium intoxication.

Cathartic Agents

Cathartic agents are rarely used in the horse. Cathartics work by irritating the intestinal wall, which causes it to secrete water. They can also directly stimulate contraction of the muscles of the intestines. Unfortunately, horses can develop chronic diarrhea from the administration of such cathartic agents as castor oil or cascara sagrada. Most veterinarians recommend therapy that is less irritating to the intestines than the cathartics.

Nasogastric Intubation (Stomach Tube)

The use of a stomach tube as a diagnostic tool was discussed in the previous chapter. Of course, a nasogastric tube is also commonly passed into the colicking horse's stomach to deliver medication.

Trocharization

As you know, horses ferment their feed in the large intestine. As a byproduct of fermentation, gas is produced. If passsage of feed through the bowel is somehow interrupted, large amounts of gas can accumulate in the intestines. The gas stretches and distends the bowel, causing pain and discomfort.

It may be possible in some horses to relieve the gas from the intestines by sticking a long needle, or trochar, into them and letting the gas out the horse's side. This is generally done through the horse's right flank, just behind the ribs. This spot is where the large intestines and the cecum are most accessible. As with abdominocentesis, the risks involved in passing a needle through the horse's side and into the intestines are minimal.

Routine precautions to ensure a clean procedure should, of course, be followed with trocharization.

ENEMA

An enema is injection of liquid into the rectum. It is a technique that is frequently used in newborn foals. These babies can occasionally have impactions of the small colon and rectum with meconium. Meconium is a dark material that forms in the intestine of the fetal horse, made up of intestinal secretions and fetal fluids.

An enema is the standard treatment for meconium impactions in foals. Very occasionally, meconium impactions can be serious enough to require surgical removal. Predictably, in an effort to prevent meconium impactions, many newborn foals are given enemas within hours of birth as part of routine neonatal care. Although there's little harm in this practice, most foals don't need it.

Many horse owners hope that an enema can relieve colic problems in the adult horse, too. Giving an enema to an adult horse is a futile effort and it's incredibly messy. An enema in an adult horse may rinse out the last three or four feet of the intestinal tract. However, problems in the intestinal tract of the adult horse occur far out of the reach of the fluid delivered in an enema. The risks to the horse of perforation of the rectum and to the veterinarian or horse owner of getting kicked by the surprised and irritated horse far outweigh any potential benefit to be gained from an enema.

Therapeutic enemas with lidocaine, a local anesthetic, have been advocated by some veterinarians as a way to stop horses from excessive straining during abdominal distress or during rectal examination. It's rarely needed.

TREATMENT OF INFECTION

For conditions in which the problem appears to be caused by bacteria or is infectious (and is accompanied by colic-like signs), antibiotic therapy may be appropriate. As previously mentioned, conditions such as pleuropneumonia and peritonitis (infections of the chest and abdominal cavities, respectively) can demonstrate colic-like signs. These conditions are most commonly treated medically. Antibiotics are a cornerstone of therapy for these conditions.

The selection of an antibiotic for a sick horse is based on a number of factors, including the severity of the condition, the infectious agent that caused the condition, the age of the horse and the metabolic status of the horse, to name but a few. The best antibiotic agent for your horse is the one that works; an antibiotic that costs one hundred dollars per day is not necessarily more effective than one that costs five dollars per day; nor is the cheaper antibiotic the best choice if the horse is going to die because of your attempts to save money.

Antibiotic therapy may also be prescribed for your horse if it is felt that surgical intervention may be needed to correct his colic problem. Antibiotics alone have increased the survival rate of horses with experimentally induced intestinal obstructions. In addition, if the horse has antibiotics in his system when he is operated on, it may help decrease the incidence of postoperative infections.

OTHER MEDICATIONS

A number of other drugs are occasionally used in the treatment of specific conditions associated with colic, most particularly during or after colic surgery. Such medications are rarely, if ever, used in the initial treatment of the colicking horse and so will not be discussed at length in this book. These drugs include:

- Those that attempt to help stimulate motility of the bowel, such as metaclopramide, bethanecol, erythromycin, yohimbine and neostigmine. These drugs are not always effective and many have undesirable side effects. These side effects include abdominal pain due to uncoordinated contractions of the intestines, stumbling and incoordination.

- Those that attempt to improve the function of the cardiovascular system. If horses are in shock, drugs such as dopamine and dobutamine can be used, in conjunction with intravenous fluids, to increase the output of the heart and to help maintain circulation.

- Dimethyl sulfoxide (DMSO). DMSO is a solvent that is used in an incredibly large number of conditions in the horse because of its anti-inflammatory properties. Its method of action is not well understood. However, DMSO is thought to help remove chemicals that are produced during inflammation and after tissue has had its blood supply reduced (such as when the intestines twist; the tissue is said to be ischemic). As such, DMSO is given by some veterinary surgeons during colic surgery in order to try to help horses recover from the adverse effects of lack of tissue blood supply. Unfortunately, one study done on DMSO failed to show any beneficial effect in protecting intestines from the adverse effects of ischemia.

Chapter 7

Surgical Colic

THE DECISION TO PERFORM COLIC SURGERY ON A HORSE is rarely an easy one. Even if the veterinary indications for surgery are fairly straightforward, the emotions of the horse owner, cost of the surgery and risks to the horse are all factors that must be considered before deciding whether a horse with colic should be operated on.

It can be helpful to think about these things in advance, when such a decision isn't a matter of life and death. It is unlikely that an individual horse will ever need colic surgery. There are many, many things to consider if he does. A checklist of questions to weigh include:

1. If your horse were to need surgery, could you afford it? Colic surgeries can cost many thousands of dollars. If that kind of money isn't something you can part with easily, perhaps you might consider an insurance policy that helps pay for colic surgery or major medical problems.

2. Is your horse insured? Insurance companies require notification that a horse is going to have colic surgery and most must approve

treatment or, if necessary, euthanasia. Keep the telephone number of your insurance company where you can find it.

3. Do you have a trailer? When your horse is sent to the hospital, he will need to be moved immediately. If you have the ability to move your horse, great. If not, make sure you know the name and telephone number of several people who might be able to help haul him to the hospital on short notice.

4. Do you know the directions to the closest surgical facility, the one where he can get the most immediate care? Do you have its telephone number?

Once the major decision has been made to perform surgery, your horse's life rests in the hands of the surgeon. He or she is the person most qualified to make the decisions that may save your horse's life. Colic surgery is a major effort, made even more dramatic by the size of the horse and the emotional attachments of those involved with the horse. Even so, advances in veterinary medicine and care have made colic surgery a well-accepted and well-defined procedure. Many horses that would have died even a few years ago can be saved because of advances in techniques and equipment that make colic surgery and anesthesia a quicker and safer undertaking than ever before.

Many people fear that if a horse has a surgery for colic he will be somehow permanently weakened or impaired. In general, this isn't true. Unfortunately, some horses do not do well after colic surgery and some do not survive their problems. However, most horses that recover from surgery do just great. They return to their normal careers and function at their presurgery levels. The fact is, if your horse needs colic surgery and he doesn't get it, he won't be able to do anything ever again. Surgery can give him a chance to come back.

Still, colic is fatal to some horses. For many reasons, it would be helpful for owners and veterinarians to have some idea of the likelihood of a particular horse surviving surgery. This would save needless suffering for the horse and needless expenditures of time and money by the owners and veterinarians.

Several studies have tried to develop methods of predicting survival from colic surgery. In a recent study conducted in Virginia with 165 horses, a method of predicting survival was developed. This method involved collecting 32 individual pieces of clinical information from each horse. The overall accuracy of the test in predicting death or survival was 93 percent—not perfect, but extremely useful. It's the best prognostic test that has been developed so far. The most useful pieces of information in helping to assess survival from colic were the following:

1. Pulse rate. On average, a pulse rate of about 73 beats per minute or more is a bad sign. Horses with pulse rates of about 53 beats per minute or less on average tend to survive.

    If a horse's pulse is racing, it may indicate that his cardiovascular system is in trouble. With shock, or with compromise of the blood supply to the intestines (such as with a twist), various organ systems lose their blood supply and begin to die. The heart may start beating furiously in what can be a futile effort to try to get blood delivered throughout the horse's body.

2. Total protein concentration in the abdominal fluid. When fluid is obtained from the abdomen by abdominocentesis, the amount of total protein in the fluid can be quickly measured. Average total protein levels of 3.5 are associated with a poor prognosis. Average levels of 2.5 or below are associated with horses that survive.

3. Blood lactate concentration. Lactate concentrations are a measurement of the amount of lactic acid in the blood. Excessive amounts of lactic acid are produced in situations where the body's metabolism is functioning without the presence of oxygen (this is called anaerobic metabolism). In colic, increases in blood lactate indicate

that the horse is in shock and that parts of his body aren't receiving enough oxygen.

Average blood lactate concentrations of 58.3 or greater are associated with a poor survival from surgery. An average concentration of 23.9 or less is a good prognostic sign. Unfortunately, this test cannot be done in the field.

4. Abnormal mucous membranes. An abnormal color of the mucous membranes is associated with horses that do not survive their colic episodes. Horses with normal mucous membrane color tend to do well. Like the heart rate, the color of the mucous membranes reflects the cardiovascular status of the horse.

Once the horse is prepared for surgery and anesthetized, the surgeon will make an incision along the middle of the abdomen and begin his or her exploration. Most good colic surgeons have developed their own method of rapid exploration of the abdomen and are usually able to identify the problem relatively quickly. Occasionally, if the problem is recognized quickly enough, the surgeon is able to fix things merely by returning segments of bowel to their normal positions. In more complicated cases, once the problem causing the colic has been identified, there are several techniques that may be performed to straighten things out.

DECOMPRESSION

The large intestines tend to produce a lot of gas, a by-product of the bacterial fermentation in this part of the bowel. During surgery, gas-filled segments of large intestine can balloon out of the abdominal incision, making exploration of the abdomen or return of the bowel to the abdomen difficult. Trying to put gas-filled intestines back into the abdomen is like trying to stuff extra clothes into a suitcase.

Therefore, the surgeon may elect to decompress the bowel. Decompression means to suck the gas out of the intestines. This is done by sticking a needle in it to let the gas out. It's sort of a direct trocharization procedure. The process can be sped up by using a machine to suction the gas. The needle puncture in the bowel seals within seconds. Decompression poses little risk to the horse and has a lot of benefits.

Enterotomy

An incision into the bowel is called an enterotomy. If there is an obstruction in the intestines, an enterotomy may be performed, usually next to the obstruction, in an area of healthy bowel. The incision is made into healthy bowel so that when the incision is sewn up, it will be more likely to heal without problems. Then, the obstruction can be carefully removed through the enterotomy incision.

Enterotomies are also used to help evacuate the intestines of contents such as sand or large amounts of feed. An incision can be made in the bowel and a garden hose (believe it or not!) can be introduced inside to rinse out the contents of the intestines. The enterotomy incision is then closed, using either sutures or mechanical stapling equipment. Next, the incision is cleaned and the bowel is returned to the abdomen. Enterotomy is a fairly straightforward procedure.

Resection-Anastomosis

Sometimes, as a result of the intestines being twisted or trapped in an abnormal position, a portion of the horse's intestines may die. The effect of trapping a portion of the intestines or twisting it tightly is just the same as if you were to put a rubber band around the end of your finger: tissue dies. If you remove the rubber band from your finger quickly enough, there will be no problem. If you leave it in place for too long, the end of your finger will die because of the tissue damage and death caused by the lack of blood circulation.

When death of a segment of intestine occurs, sometimes the dead or dying segment can be removed. This procedure is called a resection. Of course, the two ends of healthy intestine that remain have to be sewn (using suture material that is absorbed by the body) or stapled (using a mechanical stapling device) back together; this technique is called an anastomosis.

A surprisingly large amount of intestine can be removed from the horse with little ill effect. For example, almost the entire jejunum, or essentially the whole large colon, can be removed from a horse if his colic condition warrants such a dramatic surgery. Sometimes, however, the damage caused by impairment to the circulation of the intestines is so extensive that it is not possible to leave enough healthy bowel in the abdomen to support the horse's life. Sadly, in this circumstance, a horse must be euthanized on the surgery table.

Colostomy

A colostomy is a surgical technique that is occasionally employed in the treatment of rectal tears in the horse. A rectal tear is a very serious condition. Fecal material can pass through the tear and contaminate the abdomen. Unfortunately, the rectum is not an area that is easily reached through an incision in the horse's abdomen. Sometimes a rectal tear just can't be sewn back together.

A colostomy diverts the small colon to a surgically created opening in the abdominal wall. Fecal material then passes through the colostomy opening. While the colostomy is in place, the torn rectum heals on its own (the body's capacity for healing is really remarkable), without the interference of the movement of fecal material. After a few weeks, the colostomy opening is closed and the segments of the intestines are reunited.

A colostomy is not an easy surgery and management of a horse with a colostomy is best done in a hospital. There can be many complications of this surgery, such as infection of the abdominal cavity, stricture (narrowing) of the surgery site and failure of the procedure. However, colostomy has been effective in treating some severe rectal tears of the horse.

Colopexy

Colopexy is a procedure advocated by some veterinary surgeons in an attempt to help horses that have had one or more episodes of torsion of the large colon. In this surgery, the wall of the colon is partially divided and sewn to the lining of the abdominal cavity. The hope is that the bowel will heal to the wall of the abdomen and consequently become fixed in position. This could conceivably prevent the mobility that allows for torsion of the large bowel.

Colopexy is not a surgery without problems. It can be difficult to perform a colopexy on intestines that have had their blood supply compromised by a twist. Even in healthy horses, a colopexy is not a trouble-free procedure. Still, in horses that have had repeated twists of their large colons, some preventative procedure such as colopexy or large colon resection may be considered.

CHAPTER 8

Colic Surgery: The Aftermath

Ideally, after colic surgery, the horse will begin to eat, drink, defecate and do all the normal things that horses do. The horse will be monitored at the hospital for a period of time after surgery. If there are no complications after the operation, the horse should be able to return home within one to two weeks. After that, a longer period of time, usually around ninety days, will be needed to allow for the incision in the horse's abdominal wall to heal. Although the abdominal wall should be strong enough to withstand riding stresses and normal activity within ninety days, healing and strengthening of the wall actually continues for as long as a year after surgery!

Unfortunately, not all colic surgeries go smoothly during the recovery phase, although the majority of them do. As with any surgical procedure, complications can arise. Some of them are life-threatening or even fatal. Even with the best surgical care, some of the postsurgical complications may not be avoidable.

All surgery has risks that come with it. The more damage to the intestines that existed prior to surgery and the more metabolic complications that existed prior to surgery, the more likely that problems will occur after surgery. In some horses, however, even with the best care and early intervention, things can go wrong. Often, no one knows why.

The best way to avoid complications after surgery is to have the horse operated on as quickly as possible after the problem is identified. After surgery, the horse should be monitored carefully and any problems that arise should be addressed quickly and aggressively.

ILEUS

Sometimes the intestines do not react kindly after the surgeon has invaded the abdomen and handled or cut them. Ileus is a paralysis of the normal muscular movement of the intestines from the mouth to the rear. It is a common complication of surgery, especially after surgery of the small intestine. Usually, if surgery is performed quickly with a minimum of handling of the abdominal contents and the horse is given good postoperative care, the intestines will eventually begin to move. Until they do, however, there can be a lot of anxious moments for the attending veterinarians. Unfortunately, ileus does not respond consistently to any type of drug therapy. It may be necessary to continuously remove fluid from the horse's stomach via a nasogastric tube until movement of the bowel resumes.

The longer that ileus remains, the greater the likelihood of secondary problems such as peritonitis or adhesions. Sometimes, in spite of all medical efforts, a second surgery may even be required to correct problems that occurred because of the first surgery.

Ileus can be a real postoperative problem. There is no good therapy that has been developed to consistently prevent or treat it.

SHOCK AND ITS COMPLICATIONS

The term *shock* describes a condition characterized by collapse of the horse's circulatory system. Shock can be a feature of many diseases causing colic in the horse. The complications of shock can be difficult to treat in the horse after surgery. Such things as pre- and postoperative antibiotics and fluid therapy, which are used to deter infection and dehydration, can also be useful in preventing shock and other postoperative complications. However, even with proper postoperative care, shock is an ever-present, though fortunately rare, threat to a horse with severe metabolic complications. Conditions associated with shock and infection include:

1. Thrombophlebitis, which is an inflammation of the veins with the formation of blood clots. The most frequently affected vein is usually the jugular vein.

   In sick, shocky horses, tubes known as catheters are inserted into a horse's vein (usually the jugular vein of the neck) to allow for continuous intravenous therapy without continual puncturing of the vein with needles. Catheters, however, can be a double-edged sword. Catheters in the veins can rattle around and irritate the veins themselves. In shock or after infection, the surface of irritated veins can begin to form blood clots and become inflamed or infected. Aggressive therapy is mandatory for resolution of this problem.

2. Disseminated intravascular coagulation (DIC), which is a condition characterized by abnormal clotting of the blood. Fortunately, this is a very rare complication associated with abdominal surgery. DIC is most frequently seen with shock that occurs as a result of peritonitis or intestinal infection and enteritis. Treatment of this condition is very difficult and development of DIC is a grave sign.

3. Kidney failure. Failure of the kidneys to perform their normal function of filtering the blood can ultimately be fatal to the horse. Shock can reduce the delivery of blood to the kidneys and impair their ability to function. Even some of the drugs used to treat colic, such as nonsteroidal anti-inflammatory drugs and a class of antibiotics called aminoglycosides, can have adverse effects on the kidney. The bad effects of these drugs on the kidney are further increased if the horse is in shock or dehydrated. Treatment with large volumes of intravenous fluids is important for the resolution of kidney problems.

LAMINITIS

Laminitis is a serious problem that faces some horses in the immediate postsurgical period. All horses with disease of the intestines are susceptible to laminitis; no one yet knows the exact causes or reasons why a few unfortunate horses develop this serious condition.

Laminitis (founder) is an inflammation of the tissues that connect the sensitive living tissues of the foot to the overlying dead hoof. Laminitis causes pain and inflammation of the horse's feet and it can have devastating consequences, in terms of both the horse's future soundness and his immediate survival. Discussion of all of the therapies for laminitis are beyond the scope of this book.

COLITIS/ENTERITIS

Colitis and enteritis are infectious and/or inflammatory conditions of the horse's intestines. (Not all inflammatory conditions are caused by infections, but all infectious conditions are accompanied by inflammation. For example, you can hit your thumb with a hammer and make it inflamed; it may not be infected.) These are difficult conditions that sometime develop postsurgery.

Colitis or enteritis can cause horses to develop severe diarrhea. These horses must be treated with large volumes of intravenous fluids to prevent dehydration and death. Laminitis is also frequently seen in horses that develop intestinal inflammation.

ADHESIONS

Adhesions are fibrous bands of tissue that cause tissues to stick to each other. They are a troubling complication of abdominal surgery. Even after the intestinal problem has been corrected, postsurgical adhesions may prevent normal functioning of the intestinal tract. Postoperative adhesions can also cause additional colic signs. In severe cases of adhesion formation, a second surgery to attempt to reduce the adhesions may even eventually be required. Unfortunately, sometimes additional surgery only has the effect of creating more inflammation in the abdomen, with more adhesions as the result.

The prevention or reduction of adhesions is a topic for considerable discussion in both human and veterinary medicine. Quick, clean surgical techniques are the best way to prevent adhesions from forming; once they begin to form, there is not much that can be done to stop them.

One of the reasons that postsurgical adhesions may be so hard to prevent is that they may be part of the normal healing of some types of intestinal wounds. Adhesions can help seal leaks that can occur around sutures placed in the intestines, for example. Therefore, the reasons for the development of intestinal adhesions is an area that is being carefully studied in both equine and human medicine. Hopefully, good recommendations for their control may eventually be made.

STRICTURE

If, during surgery, it is necessary to remove a section of the bowel that has become dead or devitalized, the healthy segments that remain have to be put back together (resection and anastomosis). Although the procedure is fairly straightforward, sometimes the horse's body doesn't cooperate after surgery.

Performing an anastomosis is sort of like sewing two tubes together. It's not only important that the sides of the tube be united. It's also important that a good-size hole be left in the middle through which the contents of the bowel can travel. If, due to excessive inflammation and scar tissue formation, for example, the size of the hole in the middle of the bowel is reduced, feed may not be able to pass through. The stricture that results from the inflammation and scarring will eventually cause signs of colic due to impaction.

There's only one way to treat a stricture. A second surgery must be performed to remove the affected segment of the intestines and a new anastomosis performed. Fortunately, stricture is a rare complication of colic surgery.

INCISIONAL HERNIA

An incisional hernia is an abnormal opening in the abdominal muscle wall. Hernias occur when the incision that was made at surgery doesn't heal back together. An incisional hernia most commonly results after the abdominal incision has become infected. Sometimes, however, even after the best of surgical care, the incision through the muscles of the abdomen will not heal.

Incisional hernias can be repaired. Usually they are repaired with some sort of a synthetic mesh. This provides strength and support to the abdominal wall. Interestingly, incisional hernias, although they are unsightly, are not associated with any significant problems for the horse. They apparently do not pose a significant risk to his future health. One study has suggested that repair of most incisional hernias may not even be necessary.

PERITONITIS

Peritonitis, as previously discussed, is inflammation of the lining of the abdominal cavity. Surgery exposes the abdomen to the potential for contamination from the atmosphere and from intestinal contents. Sometimes, bacterial leakage into the abdomen has occurred even prior to the surgery. Leakage of the contents of the intestines through a segment of bowel that has been operated on can also cause peritonitis. Sometimes, if the surgeon feels that there has been significant contamination of the abdomen during or prior to surgery, a surgical drain is placed in the abdomen to allow the infected fluid to leak out.

Medical management of peritonitis is discussed in chapter 5.

INCISIONAL INFECTIONS

Infections of the surgical wound are a frequently observed problem after surgery. In most cases, the infections are superficial—that is, they do not involve the muscular layers of the abdomen. In these horses, the surgical wounds may swell and drain for up to several weeks before they finally heal. Superficial incisional infections usually are treated with hot compresses and antibiotics. Flushing of the draining tracts is usually not a good idea because of the potential for the fluid used in flushing to enter the abdominal cavity.

If the infection in the skin wound extends into the abdominal wall, the abdominal wall may become infected and refuse to heal. While this most likely will not mean that the abdominal contents will then fall out and get dumped out on the ground, infections of the deeper tissue layers can result in an incisional hernia.

ABORTION

With pregnant mares, owners are justifiably concerned that if the mare has surgery for colic, she will lose the fetus she is carrying. Of course, the life of the mare must be the first concern, because if you lose the mare, you lose the fetus, too.

Happily, two studies on pregnant mares indicate that colic surgery does not present a terrible risk of abortion. Approximately 80 percent of pregnant mares that have colic surgery will keep their fetuses. The 20 percent that abort appear to do so because of some of the severe complications of colic, such as shock and endotoxemia.

CHAPTER 9

Colic: Risk Factors and Prevention

As you've seen, there can be many causes for colic in the horse and there are many ways that it can be treated, depending on the condition. Therefore, it should be evident that there is no single good way to prevent every single colic of the horse. The real problem with colic is that there are so many things that can cause it.

Nevertheless, a number of studies by the veterinary community have been done in an effort to identify the risk factors associated with colic. Many more are needed. A study released in March 1995 of more than 800 horses in Texas with colic is the most recent attempt to try to identify risk factors; other interesting investigations done in previous years have also shed some light on a few of the risk factors that are associated with the incidence of colic.

Before everyone who reads these next pages gets alarmed about individual risk factors, it should be pointed out that there are a lot of factors that overlap each other when you are trying to do a study on colic. For example, if a horse on pasture colics less often than a horse in a stall (as some studies have suggested), is it because he eats more grass, gets more exercise, gets more sunshine or is exposed to more parasites (well, he really would be) than a horse that is confined in a stall? Unfortunately, the results of some studies are contradictory. Also, many of the studied factors relate to each other and are impossible to separate. The final word on what causes colic in horses is not (and may never be) in.

In addition, many things are done by horse owners in an effort to prevent intestinal colics. Some of the things make medical sense; others have little basis in medicine, fact or even common sense. While these things are done with the best of intentions, they do little to prevent colics.

RISK FACTORS YOU CAN'T DO ANYTHING ABOUT

Breed

In some studies, the breed of the horse does seem to be associated with some types of colic. Of course, the breed of the horse is one thing you can't do anything about, unless you want to sell your horse. Breeds and types that are associated with particular kinds of colic include:

- Arabian horses. Arabs seem to show up a lot in colic studies. They have a higher incidence of intestinal stone (enterolith) formation than do other breeds. Studies in Texas and Georgia have found a higher incidence of all types of colic in Arabian horses. Other studies have failed to show an increased incidence of colic in Arabian horses, however.
- Large warmblood horses. They have been overrepresented in cases of dorsal displacement of the large colon in one study.

- Standardbred horses. Stallions of this breed seem to have a higher incidence of herniation of the small intestine into the scrotum than do other breeds.
- Shetland ponies and Miniature horses. These little guys have more small colon impactions than do other breeds.
- Thoroughbred horses. Entrapment of the small intestines in the epiploic foramen was seen in greater numbers of Thoroughbreds than in any other breed, according to one study.

Sex

The sex of the horse appears to have little effect on the incidence of colic, although certain types of colics are seen more in one sex than in another. It is generally accepted that mares have a higher incidence of large colon torsion than do stallions and geldings (although no studies have proved this, as yet). Among other things, a study in Georgia concluded that mares were more likely to suffer from colon torsion if they had produced at least two foals or if they had a suckling foal at their side between 80 and 100 days of age. Of course, pregnant mares are also the only horses that are susceptible to uterine torsion.

Likewise, stallions are the only horses susceptible to entrapment of the intestines in the inguinal canal or scrotum. Of course, like the breed, the sex of the horse is something you can't do much about (unless you're talking about the process of making a gelding!).

Geography

Where your horse lives is associated with particular types of colic, although it's not always clear why. Obviously, though, colics caused by impactions of sand are seen only in places where horses are kept on sandy soil, such as southern California and Arizona. For some reason, enteroliths (stones) are most commonly seen in southern California, Indiana and Florida. You could always move if this worries you.

Weather

It seems that everyone believes that a change in the weather will cause a horse to colic. Without question, the weather is always changing and horses are always colicking. (Then again, the stock market is always changing, too, although horse owners are more likely to get colic from changes in the stock market than are horses.)

Several studies have looked specifically at the association between colic and weather. Daily barometric pressure and pressure changes and the daily temperature and temperature changes have been charted and compared with the incidence of colic. No link between colic and any of these factors has ever been found.

Age

Horses less than two years of age or greater than eleven years of age do seem to have an increased incidence of colic, according to most studies. Also, once a horse is older than fifteen, the chances that his colic condition will require surgery goes up. Of course, the only thing that you can do about a horse's age is to not own one of that particular age. Horses that are less than two years old are at greater risk for such conditions as intussusceptions, small intestinal volvulus and entrapment of intestines in umbilical hernias. Newborn foals, obviously, are the only horses at risk for impactions of the meconium. Older horses have higher frequencies of such conditions as colon torsions, entrapment of small intestines in the epiploic foramen and strangulation of the intestines by tumors, such as lipomas.

Previous History of Colic or Colic Surgery

Two studies have indicated that another factor that predisposes horses to colic is a history of colic or previous colic surgery. That is, if a horse colics once, he appears to be somewhat more likely to colic again than a horse that has not suffered a colic episode. Similarly, if a horse has had a previous abdominal surgery, he appears more likely to colic again than a horse that hasn't had surgery. This suggests that some horses may be "prone" to colic. Another study in Georgia, however, was unable to associate previous episodes of colic with a likelihood of subsequent episodes.

MANAGEMENT FACTORS (THINGS YOU CAN DO SOMETHING ABOUT)

Parasite Control

Regular deworming to control internal parasites in the horse certainly makes a lot of sense. Certainly, parasites can cause lots of problems for a horse. Heavily parasitized horses do not digest their feed well and appear unhealthy. Also, in addition to colic problems, foals with ascarid infestations (roundworms) are subject to increased incidence of pneumonia. (During a stage in their life cycle, roundworms migrate through the foal's lungs.) Intestinal parasite larvae are associated with verminous arteritis. Intussusception of the large colon is associated with the presence of tapeworms.

It is not at all clear that parasitized horses colic more often than horses that are frequently dewormed, however. Two studies have looked specifically at the relationship between deworming history and the incidence of colic. These studies have found no association between deworming and colic. That is, even though certain types of parasites are associated with certain types of colics, a clear cause-and-effect relationship between an inadequate deworming program and the occurrence of colic has not been demonstrated. However, given the availability of antiparasitic agents and the ease with which deworming is performed, it makes no sense not to take efforts to control internal parasites in the horse.

The method by which you choose to control the internal parasites of your horse does not appear to be particularly important. Numerous studies have shown that deworming agents given by oral paste, in the feed or by nasogastric intubation are equally effective, assuming that the horse is given an appropriate dose for his weight and that he gets the entire dose. Therefore, there is no apparent good reason for recommending regular nasogastric intubation of the horse to control internal parasites over other methods of parasite control.

Dental Care

Prevention of colic is one of the reasons that regular care of the horse's teeth is recommended. The teeth of a horse have long roots that are pushed up continuously during his lifetime. As the surfaces of the teeth wear against each other, during chewing, irregularities on the surfaces and the edges of the teeth can form. These irregularities, often called points, are periodically smoothed off using a large rasp called a float. Hence, floating is the term used to describe routine dental care of the horse.

Proper dental care does appear to be important to ensure normal chewing of feed. Indeed, a recent study of older horses performed at a slaughterhouse showed that many older horses had dental abnormalities which caused problems such as cuts and ulcers in their mouths. Many people fear that if a horse does not chew normally, the feed he swallows might be inadequately processed, making him more prone to colic.

The study done on 832 horses in Texas failed to show any association between dental care and colic. Like regular deworming, regular dental care should be considered as part of good management practices for the horse. But it may not be critical in the prevention of colic.

Bedding

In the Texas study, colic was not associated with the types of bedding on which horses were kept. Yet in another study in Maryland, horses that were bedded on sawdust had more episodes of colic than did horses bedded on straw or wood shavings.

Housing

Housing conditions may have something to do with colic. Studies done in Maryland, North Carolina and Georgia have suggested that confinement increases the risk of colic. Small stalls or paddocks or stall confinement for more than twelve hours a day seemed to increase the incidence of colic. In the Texas study, however, colic was not associated with the type of housing and the amount of time the horses were kept out of doors was irrelevant.

Interestingly, in the Texas study, there was an association between housing *changes* and the incidence of colic. That is, colic was significantly more likely to occur within two weeks of a change in housing of the horse. Unfortunately, it was not possible for the investigators to determine whether the increased incidence of colic was due to a change in the housing or merely because of a change in feed. (After all, it would be expected that different feed would be given at a different stables.) Still, the finding that some change in management is occasionally associated with colic is food for thought.

Exercise

Regular exercise may be an important factor in helping to prevent colic. Some studies have suggested that horses that can get out and move around, such as horses in pasture or those in riding schools, colic less. Another study, however, suggested that horses used in competitive events and in racing had the highest risk of colic. Still, it's pretty hard to argue against exercising your horse regularly. After all, that's what you got him for, isn't it?

Caretaker

Here's one for you. A joint study in Colorado and Pennsylvania suggested that a horse that is taken care of by a trainer is almost three times as likely to colic as a horse taken care of by its owner. What this means, though, is hard to say. It could be that horses that are taken care of by their owners get more exercise or are more likely to be kept in pasture than are trainer-tended horses. It could also mean that trainers keep a closer eye on horses in their care than do owners. The horse in a trainer's care may not colic more than the horse at home, but if he does colic, he may be more likely to be seen while at the trainer's. Like other aspects of colic, there's no clear-cut answer here either.

Regular Feeding

In the wild, horses spend 50 to 60 percent of their time eating. Their digestive tract is therefore presented with feed in a relatively continuous fashion. In captivity, however, horses are generally fed two to three times a day, a situation that clearly does not mimic life in their natural state. Some people have suggested that intermittent or irregular feeding of horses in captivity makes them prone to colic. Indeed, a couple of studies have indicated that horses that are kept on pasture have a decreased incidence of colic when compared to horses that are kept in stalls. However, there is also no clear indication that the method of feeding horses in captivity causes colic.

Nonetheless, horses do like to eat at regular intervals and there certainly is nothing at all wrong with taking some pains to make sure that they do. Horses kept in stalls tend to get bored easily and feeding small amounts of feed frequently may be one way to help prevent the occurrence of habits developed to help the horse pass the time, such as cribbing or stall weaving.

Cribbing, Wood Chewing, Stall Weaving and Other Vices

One commonly held belief is that horses that practice stall "vices" such as cribbing tend to colic more. When a horse cribs, he grabs hold of some object, usually his feeder or a piece of wood, and pulls back. He may also be observed to "suck air" while he's doing this. The fear of some people is that the horse will ingest the air that he's "sucking in" and be more likely to colic as a result.

There is certainly no experimental evidence to support the belief that stall vices lead to colic. (Nor is there any evidence that horses that practice stall vices will teach other horses to crib or weave. These behaviors also occur in the wild.)

As for wood chewing, it's just another thing that horses do to pass the time and to irritate their owners. Wood that is ingested by the horse isn't harmful to him; most of it is merely digested.

Feed Changes

It is a commonly held belief that when a horse is to have a feed change, such as after one load of hay runs out, the new feed should be introduced gradually, so as to help avoid any gastrointestinal upset. It's pretty hard to find anything wrong with this practice. Until recently, however, there was no experimental evidence to support the importance of this practice. In the Texas study of horses with colic, a recent change in diet was found to be significantly associated with an increased incidence of colic. About 20 percent of the 807 horses that had had an episode of colic had also experienced a change in their feed in the two weeks prior to their colic.

Feed changes certainly do not cause colic in all horses. For example, horses kept in large boarding stables never have the "luxury" of a slow introduction of new feed. There have been no reports to suggest that this is a problem in these horses. However, if you are contemplating a feed change and can make it gradually, it might be worth the effort.

Feeds and Feed Quality

Several risk factors for colic relating to feed are commonly felt to be true. An excess of grain in the horse's diet in relation to the amount of hay is thought to predispose to colic (it unquestionably predisposes a horse to being fat). A study in Maryland supports the idea that feeding grain increases the risk of colic. One study associated the feeding of pelleted grain products with displacement of the large colon.

Poor-quality hay is thought to lead to impactions of the colon and ileum. In another study, feeding pelleted hay was associated with impactions of the large colon. (This is possibly because pelleted feed passes up to 8 to 12 percent more quickly through the intestines than does hay. It's been theorized that the bacteria in the intestines may not have adequate time to thoroughly digest the pelleted feed, leading to bigger chunks of material in the bowel, which predisposes to impaction.)

The quality of the feed is certainly very important. Hay or grain that is moldy can make horses very sick. Why would you want to give your horse poor-quality feed anyway?

Water

Some veterinarians think that inadequate water intake predisposes horses to impaction-type colics. There is, of course, never any reason to limit your horse's access to water.

In cold weather, horses have been demonstrated to drink less. Also, when it is cold outside, horses will drink more water if it has been warmed first, although, curiously, they seem to prefer the colder water if given a choice (go figure). If you can supply a warmed water source for your horse in cold weather, it may be worth the trouble just to get him to drink more. (If you can't warm up his water, at least break the ice on the water trough for him.)

Water that is high in mineral content has been suggested as a cause of enterolith formation by some veterinarians. What you are supposed to do about this problem, if it is in fact a problem, is a bit harder to say, unless you want to go to the extreme (and expensive) measure of supplying bottled or deionized water for your horse.

It's commonly recommended that "hot" horses (those that have just exercised) not be given cold water, in part because of fear that the cold water will make them colic. For this reason, horses that have recently exercised are often cooled out for extended periods of time and allowed only limited access to water. Although it's difficult to argue with the practice of allowing a horse that has recently exercised to cool down slowly, at the same time, there's no medical research to suggest that it's an important factor in preventing colic.

One thing about water and exercising horses is clear; if a hot horse is supposed to continue to exercise, as in an endurance activity, it is important that he be allowed to drink as much as possible. There's no real fear of colic in these horses. The risk of dehydration and metabolic problems in a vigorously exercising horse that's deprived of water far outweighs any potential risk of colic. Endurance horses should be encouraged to drink all they can during a ride.

Feed Additives (Things That Owners Do)
Bran

Most bran is made from wheat. Bran is a commonly prescribed source of fiber in the human diet. Bran is useful in helping people stay regular in their bowel movements because it adds bulk to the diet and it absorbs and holds water in the intestines. It is therefore considered a mild laxative for people. Presumably because bran is so commonly used in people, horses get to eat a lot of bran, too.

It is difficult to imagine, however, a diet that is higher in fiber than that of the horse. Bran is a poor sister to hay when it comes to fiber content. In addition, studies have shown that even when horses are fed very large amounts of bran, there is no effect on the consistency of their manure. Nevertheless, the belief persists among horse owners that regular administration of bran to horses is a good preventive against colic.

Horses do like to eat bran. For that reason, bran may be useful in the *treatment* of colic in a couple of ways. First, a horse that begins to eat bran during a colic episode is one that may be recovering and getting over his pain. (Of course, the same thing could be said of a horse that begins to eat carrots or any other feed.) Secondly, administration of a wet bran mash may be one way to help get water into the horse's sytem. Water may help soften firm impactions of feed. Finally, the mere presence of some feed in the bowel can serve as a stimulus for normal bowel movement. You certainly don't want to go putting large amounts of bran or any other feed in behind a firm impaction or intestinal obstruction, however.

Perhaps predictably, for all those people who extol the virtues of feeding bran, there are some people who feel that feeding bran is bad. Bran is relatively high in the mineral phosphorus. Some people feel that high amounts of minerals in the horse's diet contribute to the formation of intestinal stones. In addition, feeding bran may favor an increase in the pH of the bowel (a decrease in the acidity), which is also felt by some veterinarians to be a contributing factor to stone formation. Although there is no clear benefit to feeding bran to treat or prevent colic, there's certainly no clear evidence that it's harmful to horses, either.

Mineral Oil

Some horses are given regular doses of mineral oil in their feed to keep the bowel "lubricated" (whatever that means). Other horses are given light mineral oil by nasogastric intubation prior to transport, in an effort to prevent colic during shipping.

No evidence exists to suggest that mineral oil is effective in keeping a horse from colicking. It's hard to imagine why it would be, given that mineral oil has no residual effect on the intestines after it has passed through the horse's system.

One thing is certain. Giving a horse mineral oil prior to shipping him will guarantee you a mess to clean up in the trailer.

Vinegar

Vinegar in the horse's diet is promoted by some people as a method of preventing the formation of intestinal stones. The hope here is that the enteroliths may not be able to form in an acidic environment.

In dogs, acidification of the urine by adding things like ammonium chloride to the feed is one of the common treatments to try to help prevent formation of stones in the bladder. Acidification is the key here. Vinegar added to the horse's diet has been demonstrated to make the intestinal environment more acidic. However, whether this actually helps prevent the formation of enteroliths is pure speculation.

Psyllium

Administration of psyllium in the horse's feed is an effective way to help treat accumulations of sand in the large intestines. The use of psyllium is discussed in the chapter on medical management of the colicking horse.

Unfortunately, there's no way to prevent colic in your horse. Even if your horse seems to be at increased risk for colic (according to some of the studies), there's no way that you can predict whether an individual horse is going to suffer from colic problems. The best thing that you can do for your horse to prevent a colic is to take care of him. Exercise him regularly, make sure that he gets good feed and that his medical needs are attended to. Then keep your fingers crossed.

EPILOGUE

I F YOU CAME TO THIS BOOK HOPING FOR EASY ANSWERS on how to treat and prevent colic, the author is sorry: those easy answers do not exist. If you have learned that colic is a complex problem with many possible causes and solutions, your reading has been a complete success.

Good management and feeding practices are the only things you can do to help reduce the incidence of colic in your horse. Unfortunately, even with the best of care, a colic episode may be inevitable for your friend. Once you recognize that your horse has colic, get help quickly and respond to it attentively; that is the best way to prevent many of the bad things that can happen to the colicking horse. Rely on the advice of your veterinarian for treatment of your horse with colic; he or she is a much better source of information than your friends, trainers or concerned in-laws. And, of course, now you have this book.

BIBLIOGRAPHY

Cohen, N. D., et al. "Case-Control Study of the Association Between Various Management Factors and Development of Colic in Horses," *Journal of American Veterinary Medical Association* 206, no. 5 (1995): 667–73.

Furr, M. O., P. Lessard, and N. A. White. "Development of a Colic Severity Score for Predicting the Outcome of Equine Colic," *Veterinary Surgery* 24, no. 2 (1995): 97–101.

Morris, D. D., J. N. Moore, and E. S. Clark. "Comparison of Age, Sex, Breed, History and Management in 229 Horses with Colic," *Equine Veterinary Journal Supplement* no. 7 (1989): 129–32.

Robinson, N. E., ed. *Current Therapy in Equine Medicine 2.* Philadelphia: W. B. Saunders Co., 1987.

———. *Current Therapy in Equine Medicine 3.* Philadelphia: W. B. Saunders Co., 1992.

White, N. A. *The Equine Acute Abdomen.* Philadelphia: Lea and Febiger, 1990.

Index